MW00915897

Celestial Being

HOW TO SHIFT TO FIFTH DIMENSIONAL LIVING

BY Cindy Bentley

Copyright © 2012 Cindy Bentley
All rights reserved.

ISBN: 146376183X
ISBN 13: 9781463761837

Acknowledgements

I am deeply honored to be allowed to channel divine energies for healing and transformation. I want to thank the many souls along the way who have supported and assisted me in holding the vision of divine service.

My special thanks to Steve Bentley for his love and support and to my beloved children, Catherine and Elizabeth Bentley.

Thanks to Nannie Kate Jones, my grandmother, and to Jeanette Peek, my aunt, for teaching me love and acceptance from a very early age.

For offering many hours of listening with a compassionate heart, I wish to thank Denise Mulligan Miller. She has always understood the challenges I face in stepping into higher frequencies of being and helped me to clarify the ever-changing forms of ascension in my life.

This book came into fruition through the great professional assistance of my friend Elizabeth Ireland. She continually encouraged me to keep working, to keep expanding on what I know to be the truth that needed to be shared in this format.

My thanks to those of you who read and use this book. It is my deepest wish that the information and resources that lie herein assist you on your journey of transformation.

Dedication

Thanks to Nannie Kate Jones, my grandmother, and to Jeanette Peek, my aunt, for teaching me love and acceptance from a very early age.

Foreword

Once a long time ago, a very long time ago, or perhaps it was just as long ago as it takes to blink one's eye, there existed a golden age on the planet Earth like no other time since. It was the age of Atlantis and it was Heaven on Earth. Peace and harmony reigned before it all ended in a power struggle which catapulted us into a descent into the darkness of forgetting who and what we truly are.

Atlantis was neither a paternal society nor a maternal society. It was a time when the masculine and the feminine were in balance, when people were connected, when they recognized and appreciated the value of both aspects of self in themselves and in others.

It was a time when all twelve strands of our DNA were activated and we used much more than the ten percent of our brains that we currently claim to use.

It was a time when all the kingdoms of the earth lived in harmony—the mineral kingdom, the animal kingdom, the angelic kingdom, and the kingdom of humanity. Each kingdom existed in balance with all the others. We could see and interact with the fairies, gnomes, devas, and so-called "mythical" creatures. Angels walked upon the earth. We were friends. As Atlantis split itself apart, a tremendous rupture also occurred among the kingdoms, and we made a pact that in order to protect those we loved, we would agree to forget the inhabitants of all these kingdoms, to remove ourselves from them, to make them unavailable to us. It was the beginning of duality and fear.

Currently, we are in the throes of turmoil, beginning to emerge back into the light, rediscovering the power within ourselves to create the life and the world we want. I have met many of my old friends from Atlantis who have reincarnated at this time, who volunteered with me to come to Earth, finish what we started so long ago, and help empower others during this time of transformation.

Soon, duality will cease to exist and we will emerge back into harmony with all life and understand the true concept of unity. Some of us, many of us, are either still able to connect to those kingdoms or are re-learning that ability. Perhaps you are able to do so.

Those who love plants understand their relationship with nature. They create the gardens—large or small, rooftop or patio—and invite the devas, fairies, and gnomes to play there. They hear the call of this kingdom to keep the planet clean, to recycle. Their efforts blossom and they create a small patch of heaven with a knowing that they must help to preserve our planet.

Those who love animals know how to communicate with them and receive unconditional love in return. These people heal, rescue, foster, and adopt animals who require that level of care and invite the spirit of that world to dwell with them in harmony. Many times animals help heal their caretakers and often create symbiotic relationships with their pets.

I have a special relationship with dolphins. I have always loved them, and even as a small child when visiting the beach I would sit and watch for them as they played in the ocean. Last summer I spent my vacation at the beach. My last morning was quite special for as I walked along the water's edge just after sunrise, I looked out across the water and saw a group of dolphins come up for air as they swam just off shore. I opened my heart to them and sent love energy out across the water. I so love and admire the work they do for our planet.

One lone dolphin swam with me as I walked. She stayed as close to the edge as she could, and when I stopped to send her love, she stopped and rose as if to greet me. In that moment I felt as if we knew one another.

We continued down the beach together communing and I would stop to send her love and feel her spirit as she looked at me. I acknowledged our oneness. As I neared the path for home, I did not want to leave her. I stopped to let her swim away without me and prayed for her safety, telling her I would be back and thought, oh, what a marvelous creature you are!

Those who love the angels invite them into their lives to grow spiritually, assist, and care for the well-being of all. Many of these people sense or see these Beings of Light and are able to receive and respond to their messages. Often they find what is missing in their lives by connecting to the angels. I know many who have been led down their golden pathway of purpose through that connection.

Those who love humanity learn to serve with joy. They find a way to find the best in their fellow humans and revel in that knowledge. They connect on many levels with others and truly see the divine in those they encounter. I have always felt connected to others, and my purpose has been to serve and to heal.

It is because of that love, because of that nature of Love itself that we are now preparing for the time when the veil will be lifted from our eyes. We will once again be able to see ourselves as we truly are. We will be able to heal the rupture, reconnect with all the kingdoms, and once again create the Heaven on Earth that many call the Fifth Dimension.

In 2012, the earth will cross the equator of the galaxy, an event that hasn't taken place for over twenty-six thousand years. Many changes will occur. Will it be Armageddon, the ultimate battle for the earth? Perhaps, but perhaps not. Will the earth shift on its axis, causing massive destruction in terms of volcanic activity, tsunamis, and earthquakes? That too is unknown. It could. What is certain is that we are headed for the biggest shift the planet has ever known, from the third-dimensional duality under which we have lived for so many eons to a fifth-dimensional reality of unconditional love and oneness. I believe we will expand beyond our current human knowing in ways that are difficult to describe in language.

People all over the earth are awakening to who they truly are. People all over the world are awakening to a higher consciousness. If this book speaks to you at all, you are one of them. You are re-membering—meaning you are calling the parts of yourself that have been scattered or sublimated and bringing them back together so that you can be the healer, teacher, leader, lover, loved, and loving one that you have always been, who you truly are. Part of my mission is to help you reintegrate all aspects of your self to be all you can be and encompass your courage, consciousness, and insight.

We are living at a time like no other. Other generations have been challenged and tempered by war, major geological upheavals, and economic crises in their lifetimes. We are confronting all of these challenges at the same time. Today we face a world in the throes of evolution. While every generation may think that, our generation faces that truth. Earthquakes, tsunamis, hurricanes, and cyclones have already wrought much devastation on the earth. Weather patterns are changing dramatically. Indeed, the earth has already shifted on her axis, and the poles have moved by degree. We are facing complete change—the birthing of a new earth. It is only when we step back that we can truly understand that all of these events are orchestrated to wake us up and open our hearts to one another and to the beloved planet on which we all reside.

Mother Gaia has called to me, and I have wept with her. I feel her pain, and I work to send her love and healing energy. A living organism in her own consciousness, Gaia is going through her own growth process and will expand and become that Fifth-Dimensional reality as well.

It is no accident that you are here at this time. You chose to be here. You wanted to be part of this spiritual awakening. You wanted to participate and facilitate this process. You have much to offer.

A long time ago, the Light of understanding dimmed, and the knowledge of who we truly are was lost. There have been Masters since that time who tried to remind us, reconnect us with who we truly are, but it is not until right now, this time, our time, that we have the opportunity to remember. Now we are in a cycle where our understanding is returning and expanding, and we have the opportunity to watch as the world regains the Light.

Not gradually, not over generations, but now, in a very short time, the great shift will take place and usher us into a period of peace and prosperity unknown in written history.

We are all shifting into a fifth-dimension reality, ready or not. And you have to ask yourself, as they so often do in the movies, "Do you want to do this the hard way or the easy way?"

This book will be a resource for you to allow the easy way.

If any of this resonates for you, if any of this calls to you, then you are awakening, and this book is for you.

Open the door and follow the path that leads to your soul. Welcome to your journey home to Celestial Being.

Introduction

We are here to co-create Heaven on Earth. This is both an exciting and trying time in the planetary ascension process. Consciousness must evolve ever more quickly. Every day brings more opportunities for becoming more awake and in love with spirit as well as more opportunities for confusion and limitation. We are completely at choice about what we make **real** in our lives. Every decision we make affects the ascension process, as do everyone else's.

Thousands of years ago our DNA was disassembled. Split apart, *unplugged*. It began to broadcast within only a limited frequency. The twelve original strands of DNA were left within the human cells, yet only two remained active; the rest were not functional. This is why scientists call about 98 percent of our DNA "junk DNA" because it is dormant and has no known purpose.

It is not without purpose. Human cells have light-encoded filaments that carry information and light connecting us to our Divine Creator. However, because of that genetic engineering, we lost our conscious connection to the God/

Goddess within. Our consciousness began to be based on fear and the concept of duality which is third dimensional consciousness and under which we have been acting for thousands of year.

Many of us have been reincarnating here many thousands of years on this planet, our souls having originated from other solar systems or planets to come and seed Planet Earth. Now is the time that each of us as Lightworkers have been waiting for all these thousands of years. Now is the time for the healing of our DNA to connect us to the powerful Energies that are here to change our world by changing our consciousness. Now is the time for the dormant parts of our DNA to be repaired and activated to their original Divine function and purpose. Those who open themselves up to more light and love are literally having their cells and bodies rearranged and evolving into *conscious* beings of Love and Light who are great Creators.

Our twelve strands of DNA can be healed for us to be the original magnificent fifth dimensional Spiritual Beings that we were meant to be. With the healing of our DNA we should ultimately experience greater states of awareness to know who we really are. Living from our divine soul connection is different from living from our brains and mental reasoning. When we look outside ourselves we have taken the focus away from connection to our divine soul. It is time to reconnect to that divine part of us. Ultimate self-power is being divinely guided to allow and surrender to our divine guides who desire only that we live in our highest purpose.

You have this book in your hand because you opened your heart to it. The following pages offer a simple way to understand the Shift that is taking place, to get yourself in alignment with that Shift and make it as easy as possible for you to move into the next step of our evolutionary process—a spiritual one of wholeness.

You will discover an overview of the unfolding process taking place today, right now, that represents the shift in consciousness from a third-dimensional world into a fourth and ultimately a fifth dimension. You will understand the need to clear all the negativity from your past genetic coding as well as the negativity you have created in your world. You will experience tools that can help you step into a higher vibrational level in order to accommodate the Shift.

Inscribed above the doorway at the ancient temple of Apollo at Delphi and just as relevant today is the axiom "know thyself." We are aware of an inner knowing of self, and the journey to that knowing is always internal. By simply following what feels good and right to us, we are in alignment with our evolutionary process. We develop an understanding that there is much more than this physical world. Through acceptance and knowing that all is in Divine Order we create more of an opening for the higher energies to move through us. The more we practice acceptance, surrender, and allowing the easier it becomes to move forward. We become beings of Light and Love. And as we live our vibration we affect every one and every place we go. We are not only healing ourselves, but everyone in contact with our energy fields.

The entire universe will rearrange itself to accommodate our pictures of reality. As we hold these higher frequencies or vibrations we will bring information to change our world and heal our planet. This cannot be accomplished without chaos and confusion. What we observe in our outer world today is merely how our old system is being broken down to create and rebuild with **LIGHT**.

Know that you are far from alone. Millions have incarnated at this time and are on assignment to bring about the change in frequency and to assist in the rebundling of our DNA. Our DNA will evolve from two strands to twelve as we were originally created as Magnificent Powerful Beings of Light.

WE ARE the ONES we have been waiting for. We are in the Aquarian Age of the planet Earth. This is the time that each of us as Light Workers have been waiting for thousands of years.

Are you ready to evolve into the fifth dimension?

Are you ready to create a place for the Christ Energy of love and light to bring Heaven on Earth?

Are you ready to find Divine Bliss?

Are you ready to begin your journey to Celestial Being?

My prayer for you is that you find and step into the truth of who you truly are.

Namaste,

Cindy Bentley

Table Of Contents

CHAPTER ONE

You are a child of the universe, no less than the trees and the stars;
you have a right to be here. And whether or not it is clear to you,
no doubt the universe is unfolding as it should. Therefore,
be at peace with Divine Creator, whatever you conceive Him to be.
And whatever your labors and aspirations
in the noisy confusion of life, keep peace in your soul.

Max Ehrmann

A Country Girl And Her Mission

I am a Healer. I am an Energy Practitioner. I am a Sirian Lightworker. It is my mission on earth at this time to clear, cleanse, heal, and hold a higher consciousness for all with whom I come into contact. I serve by preparing others to step into the Fifth Dimension. This mission is not taken on lightly. It is felt in every cell of my being. I know who I am and what I have to do. It did not start out that way. My own journey was one of pain to one of joyous healing, and I want to share it with you.

The Lightworker

There are many Lightworkers on the planet today who are "waking up" to their Divine Mission. A

Lightworker is one who has awakened to the truth of who he or she truly is without the influence of ego. Lightworkers are dedicated to their mission and to the creation of their own inner presence and the expansion of awareness in themselves and in others.

Our mission is twofold. First it is to assist in raising the consciousness of all those on the planet today, helping to clear negative influences and hold the love and light of the Divine Creator by showing and teaching unconditional love. Secondly, we are here to assist Mother Gaia as she moves from a third-dimensional reality to that of the fifth dimension, the one of Heaven on Earth.

There are millions of us. I am only one. Perhaps you are, too. Many have awakened to their purpose and have been working at it for many years. Just think how our consciousness has been raised about the occult (hidden, or as I prefer, *metaphysical*) world in the last forty years. Everything from music, movies, television shows, psychic hotlines, astrological predictions in almost every major mainstream magazine and newspaper, books, seminars, the introduction of eastern thought, new healing modalities, and of course the abundant information on the Internet. Some of it has been very good, and some of it has been of little value. Daily we are bombarded with information that there is something "out there"—but also something *within* each one of us. So often I have heard my clients say, "I knew I had a purpose. I just couldn't find it!"

This book will speak to you of my journey as a Lightworker, how I fulfill my mission to be here at this time, why it is so important, and to offer guidance so that you may awaken and step into the all of who you truly are. I began my journey to the work I do today at a very young age.

My Early Life Framed My Consciousness

Like many of us, I grew up in a very dysfunctional family filled with pain and fear. There was fear that there wasn't enough money, that there wouldn't be enough to eat, that there would be no recourse if I or one of my four siblings became sick. I remember during the winter, freezing cold, wrapped up in covers my mother had warmed on the heater and staring down at the floorboards to the dirt beneath our house. But when I looked up through the cracked window in my corner of our four-room house, I could see the stars.

My journey through life is a spiritual one. When I was young, I wandered for hours through the woods near my home in middle Georgia. It contained a marvelous waterfall, and I spent a lot of time with an energy companion I named Birdie who met me there with other companions. They comforted me and brought me to a place of peace. These "imaginary" friends did lots of things with me—they were my true companions. They took baths with me and ate with me. They sat up in the trees in the forest and watched over me.

At first my parents humored my relationship with my invisible friends by setting a place at the table for them, often teasing me about them. Then the game got old, and they told me at five years old to grow up, live in the real world, face reality—there was no one there to help me. At the same time I dreamt dreams that came true, and my mother just didn't know what to do with her very strange child. I was so unlike anyone else.

When something occurred to upset me, I escaped to the woods where Birdie and the others met me and soothed away my sorrows. Eventually, reading became my escape and any free moment I had during the day was spent with my nose in a book. When this avenue was unavailable I would get myself out in nature following paths and creeks to spiritual adventures. I could find peace deep within a wildflower or in the sounds of running streams or as I lay in tall grasses to hide under the billowing clouds and blue skies. I understood even then that life was so much more than the adults in my life knew it to be.

I lived in a family filled with struggle and pain and loneliness. It was harsh. My parents felt that the only way to control or discipline a child was through the delivery of physical and mental pain. My mother's favorite weapon was a stick while my father's was the belt.

By the time I went to school my companions had disappeared, and I did not feel their presence in my life for many years. But I always had an urge to nurture those who were sick. Even when I was five years old if people were sick I wanted to go see about them. I brought water to them and helped them to walk. I always wanted to do something for them.

As the oldest of five children, I bore responsibilities beyond my years. I became caregiver for a mentally handicapped sister two years younger than I and then an emotionally unstable brother who was three years younger. My day-to-day existence was overwhelming. By the time I was ten, my third sibling had come along. My father worked two jobs and my mother also worked. I performed a large amount of chores as my mother could only lay her burdens on my back, too emotionally and physically drained herself to do anything else. While I was totally self-sufficient at an early age, I also keenly felt the responsibility of taking care of my mother, my siblings, and the house.

Whatever I did or tried to do was never enough to bring joy to my mother. She often said to me, "You are the most selfish person I know." I worked very hard to make her life easier and happier. It was not until I turned fifty that I finally learned that this was not possible. It was her choice to be the way she was, and I learned to let it go.

On some level I knew that education was going to be my only escape—I just didn't know how.

In order to progress, I studied at night, which was my only option. Raised in a strict Southern Baptist community, everything seemed difficult, and I questioned everything. I did not understand why the Divine Creator had sent me to such a painful place. The religion in which I was raised was one of judgment and hellfire. Accepted completely in my hometown, that particular faith caused a hardship for me because I did not accept nor did it agree with what I knew in my heart to be true. Their God sought revenge and punishment. My Divine Creator only sought unconditional love and joy.

At thirteen I remember a conversation I had with our minister, then in his early twenties, about this dichotomy. I had friends who were Catholic and Jewish. I could not believe that the Divine Creator was going to send them to hell. My Divine Creator loved everybody and there was no judgment day. I just *knew*.

I began to look around at other people's lives in my community and to question the existence of the possibility of joy. I taught myself to believe that for most people it was just fake joy. My trips to the woods happened less often. I was too busy helping to care for my siblings, convinced by those who "loved" me and thought only of my best interest, that my companions did not exist after all.

I felt such sadness, and I cried a lot. My parents fought about money quite frequently, and I would overhear their arguments. Mother was often pregnant and suffered several miscarriages. I felt as if there was something I should be doing for them. I would get so angry and frustrated with my dad because I felt like he had so much potential—I always knew things inside me—things that nobody would understand. I could see what needed to be done, but because I was a child, nobody would listen to me.

They told me, "Be quiet. Go away. If you do that again I'll hit you again—and then I'll give you something to really cry about."

The highlight of my life was my grandmother who showed me how to live. She taught me that it was okay to live outside of the box. She was my father's mother and as the second oldest grandchild, I felt I had a special place in her heart. She was a wonderful lady, and my only relief came from being in the presence of this loving grandmother who knew how to love and how to find joy.

My mother was a victim. It was so very important to me—especially as I was angry at my mother for being a victim—to have somebody in my life who wasn't a victim and someone who could give me love.

My mother's biggest insult to me as far as she was concerned was to say, "You are just like your grandmother." To me it was the highest compliment she could pay me because my grandmother truly and completely loved me.

During the summers, I continued to spend time alone. Books were a great source of comfort to me. My love of books was so strong that at fourteen years old I began writing a book entitled *My Search for Love.* I still have those first three chapters though I haven't read it in years. I also loved to fish, and sometimes my father dropped me off at a small lake on his way to work where I would fish and read all day long. I reveled in my time alone. I felt complete at the water's edge, cognizant of the nature spirits around me who offered comfort. It was heaven to be in the woods by myself in company with my loving Divine Creator.

Another highlight in my life came when I was sixteen and my youngest brother was born. It fell to me to name him so I chose Flynt after my beloved grandmother's maiden name. He became more like a son than a brother to me. A truly wonderful boy, he was gifted, brilliant, and charismatic. Eventually, he learned to play about every musical instrument, and he could sing and write music, too. Listed in *Who's Who in American Music* at fifteen, he also learned opera. He was, for all intents and purposes, my own child, and I loved him so much. When I married, he sang at my wedding, and I was so proud of him. He kept a spiritual diary about his relationship with God and urged me to do the same.

As I grew older, things began to change for me. I started dating, and when one boy expressed a special interest in me, my mother forbade me to see him. That relationship ended.

Eventually all this took a tremendous toll on me. At seventeen, I was overwhelmed with responsibilities, emotionally at the end of my rope, and clinically depressed from life in my family. I maintained straight A's in school, managed a part-time job, and had four younger brothers and sisters who needed me. I finally came to the conclusion that I could no longer bear the pain. One night I attempted suicide at a friend's house, ingesting almost every pill in her medicine cabinet. Fortunately, it didn't kill me; it just put me into a very long sleep.

When I awoke the next day, I felt hungover and consumed with sadness. I felt I had to find an answer, some support. I also realized that I was the only one with the ability to help me. Thankfully, I was guided to put myself in therapy at the local mental health clinic. I did not tell my parents what I was doing. I got friends to either lend me a car or drive me and pick me up. The therapist told me in very plain and simple terms that I was not crazy, that I just needed to get out of the stress of my home life and family and as soon as possible. He promised me everything would change after I graduated and left home. He put me on medication, but it made me fall asleep during the day in my high school classes, so I stopped taking it.

One day, I couldn't find anyone to pick me up after a therapy session, and I had to call my mother. In tremendous anger over what I was doing she told me that it was "the devil within me" and it was all *my fault*. If I was in pain, then I had done something to deserve it because God was punishing me.

The Beginning of My Work

But I knew differently. I knew that therapist was right. Somehow I found the courage to accept that within myself.

At that time, the only acceptable career paths for a woman to follow were either nursing or teaching. My cousin had become a nurse. I knew I didn't want to teach. I had always been drawn to the concept of healing, so I applied for a Nursing Scholarship at Georgia Baptist Hospital in Atlanta—the same place my cousin had gone. I received a scholarship and started school as quickly as possible the summer after high school. I was ecstatic. I was finally leaving home.

However, I was also emotionally torn. I would have to leave my two-year-old brother Flynt to my mother's care knowing that he was in for a very difficult time without me. It was traumatic for both of us because we had such a strong bond. It was awful leaving him. But I knew deep in my soul that I would be no good to him unless I was able to take care of myself first. I moved to Atlanta to become the healer that I knew in the depth of my soul I was, in the only way that was understandable and acceptable at that time.

I loved my work at Georgia Baptist Hospital. It was pure pleasure to give love and support to patients and their families. I was definitely in my bliss. I also worked at the hospital on my days off in order to make spending money. I made friends but always remained somewhat of an outsider. I was so much more mature than any of the girls in my class. No one had been raised with the kind of responsibilities I'd shouldered in my childhood. As my therapist had said, things did get better, and I felt as if I blossomed being out on my own and away from the environment in which I was raised. This was in 1969 in Atlanta—a big city with lots of young people my age. For the first time I really started to have fun.

Three Events That Changed My Life

One Sunday in 1970, during my second year in nursing school, I went shopping at a department store with some of my girlfriends. We got separated and in looking for them I went out a different entrance than the one we had entered. As soon as I stepped out of the door, I felt the sharp point of a knife stick in my back.

A tall man grabbed me and said, "Come with me and I won't hurt you."

I knew he was lying.

He put me in a car parked nearby and set me between two of his friends.

I said, "Can you just give me a ride home? I'm just two blocks away at the nursing school."

He told me no, that he wanted to take me to their house first. They took my purse, all the money I had, and all the small purchases I'd made at the store. When we got to his house he forced me into a room and locked the door. I didn't know if I was going to live or die.

For five long hours I sat in that room and prayed until he came back. I could tell immediately that he was completely strung out on drugs. I didn't know what he was going to do. I knew he was completely irrational and I felt totally at his mercy. I began to beg for my life.

Knife once again at my back, he forced me into his car. The streets were deserted now in the late Sunday afternoon, and he drove to an alley behind an office building and parked. He pulled me out of the car, and I was convinced that he was going to kill me. He wanted to rape me. Everything in my being revolted. I knew I just could not allow that and resisted.

He said, "Well, I'll kill you."

I pleaded with him for my life, and I started praying. Something seemed to shift within him, and then he decided I should engage in oral sex on him. Praying and crying I obliged, hoping all the while that he would just let me go. It must have released some of the rage within him because he relaxed somewhat, put me back in the car, drove me to my school, and let me go. My life had been spared, and it was a miracle. Much later I found out that his next victim had not been so fortunate; he had murdered her. However, I thanked the Divine Creator for sparing my life.

Back at school, I was a total wreck. Not knowing what else to do, I called my mother and told her I could not stay at school because I was "just not right." There was no way I could bring myself to tell her what had happened to me. She came and got me, and I stayed home for one full semester and worked at a nearby nursing home caring for the elderly. During that time I prayed to the Divine Creator to teach me to heal.

The psychological stress of what had happened to me was overwhelming, and I could not sleep.

When I told my mother I couldn't sleep at night and was having problems, she merely said, "Well, I've got a bottle of Valium on the top of the China cabinet—just take that when you can't sleep." Neither she nor anyone else in my family ever asked me what had happened to me.

My boyfriend at the time came to visit me, and when I finally confided in him, he made me go to the police and report the incident. I took the detective to the house where I had been held. He knew exactly where it was and what was going on, and I identified the person who had abducted me. There was a preliminary trail. I had no contacts, no legal representation, no money, and it turned out the man who'd abducted me was from a very wealthy family. They hired a high-profile attorney. When I was called to the witness stand, his lawyer made it look like I had instigated the entire incident and it was completely my fault. It was incredible—humiliating and debilitating. Consequently the man, who had abducted me, threatened me, intended to kill me at knifepoint, and physically violated me got off completely free. The detectives I worked with were dumfounded. They simply could not believe it.

At this time, while I was at home, my favorite cousin, who grew up living next door to me, died of meningitis. He was only twenty-two years old. It was another blow to my fragile system, but I was determined to return to school. Once more driven to the very limit of my endurance, I managed to help myself by going to the school counselor who got me into therapy. At these sessions all I could do was cry, but I was fortunate enough to find someone who eventually helped me and I began to make progress. I was able to return to classes and work toward finishing my education.

The following year, a district attorney in Florida contacted me to tell me that the same man who had been accused of abducting and molesting me had killed an eighteen year-old girl. He wanted me to come to Florida and testify. Still in therapy at the time, my therapist said I was much too fragile and that I would not be able to handle facing or testifying against this man once again. I told the district attorney that his family was very wealthy and that I was convinced that if I testified not only would I be humiliated by their legal representation, but I would be in fear for my own life. I could not put myself through a repeat of the last trial experience I had had.

The next incident that propelled me into understanding my mission occurred shortly after graduation. I was offered a position as charge nurse working nights in the pediatrics department at Georgia Baptist. I had almost a perfect score in pediatrics on my finals. I understood children and had cared for them my whole life to that point. I also liked being with children. Their innocence and ability to love without blocking their emotions appealed to me on several levels. As adults people block love because they don't feel deserving of love, but children soak it in.

On that floor we had children with cancer and other terminal illnesses. It was the 1970s, and changes and strides in medicine for children had not peaked yet. Several beautiful children took their last breath as I held them in my arms. In addition, Hospice care was not an option—indeed it did not even exist at the time.

I remember one beautiful eleven-year-old boy named Bobby who suffered from cancer for two years. One night I heard him call my name at three in the morning.

"Cindy, Cindy, come hold me. I am falling."

I held him close, but not close enough as he kept telling me that I needed to hold him tighter, that he was still falling.

The minute he fell into that other world beyond this veil of illusion, I wanted to call "code blue," but his mother held my arm and said, "No, he has suffered enough."

Once again I prayed to the Divine Creator to teach me to heal. There were other children in that department who were the victims of terrible automobile accidents as at that time cars were not equipped with either seatbelts or car seats. Many of those children died in my arms as well.

One night just before I reported for work I drove behind the building where I lived and parked my car. As I opened the door, a man appeared from nowhere, knocked me to the ground, and started shooting me at point-blank range. One bullet went through my ear lobe and singed my hair; another went through my chest and into my shoulder; a third passed through my leg. I threw up my hands and received burns between each finger of my left hand where the bullets flew between my fingers.

When my attacker ran out of bullets, he turned and bolted down the street. Operating on pure adrenaline, in a rage that filled me so strongly and so completely, I jumped up and started to run after him. Suddenly I realized I was bleeding. I marshaled all my remaining strength and walked across the street to the emergency entrance of the hospital where I worked.

I was immediately recognized as a former student.

Greeted with, "Hey Cindy, how are you?" I replied, "I'm not really right. I have been shot."

Knowing I was safe, I collapsed on the floor as the staff went into overdrive. They immediately put me on stretcher and started to cut my clothes off to find the extent of the bullet wounds. They called in a surgeon who was one of my class doctors.

It was a miracle that even though the assailant had fired at point-blank range, none of my wounds were life threatening. My right earlobe had to be reattached, and another bullet had gone straight through the upper portion of my right thigh but had not hit the bone. The third bullet is still lodged in my right shoulder as a permanent reminder of that encounter. I now know higher beings and angels protected me and prevented the bullets from causing any real permanent damage.

That night I slept in a room on the first floor of the hospital right beside the patio. It meant that anyone could access my room through the window. I was consumed with fear that the family of the man who had victimized me had hired somebody to come and finish me off so that I could not testify. My body would not stop shaking. My brother, who was three years younger than I and now in college, happened to be in Atlanta, and he came and slept in a chair by the door to keep me safe. The next day when my doctor arrived on rounds, I explained to him that it would be best if I were moved to another room. I was twenty-one years old and had no idea if this had been a random act or intentionally planned. For the next thirty years my preservation instincts went into overdrive if I heard a loud sound or someone showed up unexpectedly at my door.

My family found out about what happened because it made the news that night. But I never spoke to anyone in the family about the abduction or about the shooting, and no one ever asked. My understanding from my upbringing was that if you were in pain it was because you deserved to be in pain; you deserved to be punished by God. That was their understanding, and I knew it would be futile to tell them my story as they would place all blame back on me. At that time I lived in a world where God punished you—so everybody was a victim. Thankfully, I am now far removed from that illusion. However, because of these two experiences, I have a very deep compassion for people who see themselves as victims.

Very slowly I healed physically and eventually returned to therapy and to nursing. It turned out that the man who shot me did so as a random event. I was simply in the wrong place at the wrong time. He had only been out of prison for a week but during that time he had committed all sorts of crimes including abducting and abusing one woman, killing another for her car, and shooting me. When I showed up to identify him, the other victims of his crimes could not believe that he had shot me three times in order to steal my overnight bag.

Upon returning to work, I tended to many sick, injured, and dying children. It was there that I began to learn more about unconditional love. I began to study metaphysics, searching for answers. The more I studied, the more my understanding expanded, but I felt I was still very far from the knowledge I sought. A deep sadness set in as I observed so many sick and dying infants and children. My prayer once again was "Divine Creator, teach me to heal."

The one great joy of my life was my beloved baby brother, Flynt, sixteen years younger than I. By the time he was in his teens he traveled doing teen ministry, singing and performing Christian musicals for teenagers. When I found myself in a funk, he gave me great advice.

He said, "Cindy, what you need to do is start going to church or find someplace with positive energy. You start with that and with that one little seed, it builds."

He was only sixteen at the time, and he kept a spiritual diary. I followed his advice and joined a church where I found a group of people who eventually became friends. While I never could bring myself to believe the doctrines of that particular church, I did find the welcoming contact with people who offered support to me.

By the time I was thirty, I was still lonely and felt I needed a partner to share my life. At that time I came into contact with and was studying the principles of Unity and Science of the Mind. So I wrote down exactly what I wanted in a husband and then put it away, forgetting all about it. Within weeks, men who were not for my highest good started to leave my life. I was open and ready to meet my husband.

Today people want to be loved, want to experience the divine relationship that is possible when you are loved. Loneliness is very discouraging. However, once you learn to love yourself, once you learn to have a good time with yourself, you will attract other people to you. Think about it, people want to be around someone who is fun and having a good time with and just being who they are. I hear so much pain around finding one's "soul mate" or "twin flame."

Accepting this philosophy for myself, I made a choice to have a partner. It was not much later that I met the man I married when he visited his father on the orthopedic floor on which I then worked. When he came to my home to pick me up for our first date, he noticed the Unity books that I studied and told me his father studied Unity also!

The last event which propelled me into my healing work occurred when my beloved brother Flynt got very sick while he was in the seminary in Jackson, Mississippi. One day our mother called to tell me that the school doctor had called her and asked her if Flynt was just trying to leave school.

She 'd replied to the doctor, "My son does not want to be home—he enjoys being at school."

Without delay I called Flynt, and he said, "I'm sick."

Immediately I left work and flew to Jackson where I found my beautiful, vibrant, loving brother dying.

He spit up blood as he said to me, "Cindy, it's not fair for God to do this to me. Here I am, I'm only nineteen years old and have my whole life ahead of me. I want to have a family and do so many things and I'm dying."

I held him in my arms, and I prayed. I asked my loving Divine Creator to please teach me how to heal; I prayed to use me as a healing vessel in order to bring in His powerful healing energies and save my beloved brother.

The school doctor told me that Flynt had leukemia. I managed to get him on a flight to Atlanta the next day and into Emory hospital. Once there, our parents came in, and I left for a short while. When I returned they had moved Flynt to ICU. Mother was convinced they were not going to let me in to see him.

I simply said, "Oh, yes they will." The doctor thought I was his mother because my parents had not been very assertive with his care, so he would approach me to talk. When I walked in, there were several nurses and doctors surrounding him putting catheters and IVs into him.

He was very restless and immediately I went over to him.

He never opened his eyes, but he rose up a little and said, "Sister, are you here?"

And I said, "Yes, I'm here." I took him in my arms and told him to relax, just to take deep breaths.

He took two very deep breaths, and then he didn't breathe anymore.

An autopsy revealed that he had bone cancer. It was so extensive that they could not determine the primary site of his cancer—it had completely taken over his body. I was bereft. I searched my soul for why all I had learned about healing had not allowed me to save my own baby brother.

I did not know it then, but later came to understand that this was the final event that caused me to learn that I couldn't be of true service to myself or anyone else until I was able to heal myself. I had to learn to let go and cleanse myself of any and all negative energies so that I could heal myself and then others. I learned my most important lesson which was I could heal only as much as I was healed. I had to learn to increase my vibrational frequency in order to hold a higher unconditional love in my energy fields before I could be of service to anyone else.

A New Start

Flynt's death was unbelievably traumatic for me, and I was sad for a very long time. Then I was offered the use of a friend's condo in Cancun. My husband and I thought it was just the thing we both needed. The time we spent there was miraculous. In Mexico, I visited Chichén Itzá, and it was a very moving experience for me. There were places in Chichén Itzá that felt familiar to me. I knew I had been there before and I could *feel* the energies.

Later, I remember being in the water in Cancun and seeing a bright light. It was as if crystals were refracting light in the water, and I was one with that light. It was the most wonderful feeling I'd ever had to that point. The experience made me feel as if I were part of something much bigger than myself and at the same time feeling one with it. Seeing that one light—I will never forget it as long as I live—and feeling that feeling and knowing that light, the energy and the essence of it all. It was if in that moment I remembered a great Presence that lived within me. It was indescribable. It was wonderful.

When I got home I found out that I'd become pregnant while I was in Cancun. My husband and I had been trying to conceive for a couple of years and it seemed a miracle. Flynt had died on September 15 and by the end of October, I was pregnant.

So often with death there is new life. So it was in my life. My brother died, and I became pregnant. My father became sick, and shortly after the birth of my first daughter, he died. My paternal grand-father died a few months later, and then two years after that, my favorite grandmother died. Each of them had a form of cancer. There was so much death in my life. There had to be a reason. I had to know.

It was not until sometime later that I learned that all of these events in my life were planned. This was purposeful pain for the growth of my soul, to teach me how important it is to step into my divine mission. I continued to study metaphysics. As I studied and learned, I progressed in my career while working for a large hospital in Atlanta.

In 1995, I attended my first women's retreat at my church. During several meditations, the Archangel Michael came to me, and it was as if he was standing right in my face, pushing me to do more. If you know anything about the archangels, Michael is in charge of the Lightworkers. I kept telling him that I could not step into my mission yet because I had two little girls to raise. I asked him to please wait and I would be ready when they were older and out of school.

At one point I developed back problems and felt a deep ache in all of my bones. I was referred to a holistic chiropractor. He told me that my adrenals were "blown out" and ordered supplements for me to take. He performed a series of back adjustments and then "cleared" out the "negative entities" in my energy fields. He told me that I was being worked on by higher beings because I was to do special work, that I had the gift to heal others. I was to drink a lot of water—a gallon a day or more. I had never heard of such a thing, but I felt great. However, it only lasted for a few days. I knew I had to learn how to clear my own energy fields, and I prayed for an answer.

I discovered a book called *The Fountain of Youth* which detailed the Five Rites—yoga exercises developed by Tibetan Buddhist monks designed to open the Chakras and bring in divine energies. For the past twenty years I have performed these exercises each morning and when finished I say, "I surrender to my higher self."

Curious about healing energies, I pursued anything and everything I heard about different modalities, eventually learning to become a Reiki master.

My True Calling

It wasn't too long before I saw an advertisement for a class on dowsing which read Learn to Dowse and Keep Your Energy Fields Clear. I knew that class was the answer to my prayer. I became a master dowser and continue to use it as a tool in my work. The teacher of the class offered more extensive classes from her home, and I began to learn from her.

She felt it was her mission to be part of the work of ridding the earth of all darkness and to train others to help her. She gave me a foundational knowledge to build my healing work. By helping me to reveal more of my gifts it was possible for me to open up to my true Divine Mission. She worked to convince me of my need to assist the earth and its inhabitants of ascending into higher states of consciousness.

I also read a book by Ann Brewer called *The Power of Twelve*. It is concerned with the reconnection of our DNA strands that had been deactivated from higher consciousness and divine connections. My teacher took a course from Ann Brewer and offered to teach me as well. She called me a Sirian Lightworker who "needed to clear the dark from my soul and energy bodies to know the truth of my mission and who I am." It was at this point that my transformation began.

I started an extended apprenticeship which led me to understand who I am in the very fiber of my being. It became apparent to me that my mission is to clear and heal others. I learned how to clear myself. I witnessed miraculous healings and then began to practice healing utilizing and working with higher energy levels to relieve the suffering in those experiencing sickness, blockages, and lack. I know I could not have the compassion I possess for the people I work with had I not lived through the traumas of my own life and come to my own healing of them.

Once my children were ready for college, it was time for me to step into my real work. The week my youngest daughter went to college I once again felt the presence of the Archangel Michael pushing me forward. I didn't see him, but I felt him in every fiber of my being and in every breath I took. I *knew* he was there. I could feel how big his energy was, and I could hear him. He told me that I had to do this work. I tried to put him off again because I had a great job with benefits and money, and yet he continued to push me to take on my healing work, to step up and step out. What was I going to do? There came a point when I couldn't tell him no. He pushed all my buttons so hard that I knew it would be better for me to leave the planet then to feel the pain of not moving forward.

I found myself in the midst of what I thought was a normal world into which I always had to fit. The pain of that burden began to be too much, and I felt a strong desire to leave the world because I could no longer bear the pain. One day while I drove my car I felt the impulse to pull my car in front of a truck or just drive off a bridge. It was so difficult to explain to my husband this feeling that I was dying—unless I could do what I so strongly felt was my purpose for living.

Once again I sought counseling and was grateful to be referred to someone who understood sensitives like me. She told me it sounded like I just needed to create a business card and get on with my work. The support I felt was overwhelming. It was a seemingly simple solution, but I could not see it until I met with her. I did as she advised, and relief flooded through me that I was actually going to start my true work.

I left my career in nursing to devote myself full-time to clearing and healing the energy fields of those who come to me. Today I am in my bliss. I have worked with hundreds on a one-to-one basis and in the process have grown stronger and stronger in my own ability to fulfill my mission. I continue to take classes and work with other Lightworkers to heal myself and the planet in preparation for what is about to take place in 2012.

I believe that each and every one of us is an energy being vibrating at a certain frequency. My work is to allow each energy-being to vibrate at his or her highest frequency in order to raise consciousness to the highest level possible and step into all it is possible for that person to be. I continue to find higher energies and healing for myself so that I can channel the highest healing energies possible for others.

In order to perform this work, I must hold the highest frequency possible to show others where to go. In 2010, I met Tricia McCannon who clearly saw a matrix built around me connecting me to the higher divine beings of the sixth dimension. These beings are the ones who assist me in my work, and it is through this matrix that they are able to download what I need into my energy fields.

It is no good to say, "I want you to be just like me." I believe each person is an individual spark of the Divine Creator and must use his or her own senses to see, hear, and **feel energy**. Because of my willingness to listen and follow my heart to find my bliss I have a thriving energy practice, helping many to step into their divine pathway. I know it is a lifelong project to work on one's self, and my fundamental belief is that I cannot heal others any further than I have healed myself. My life is one of continual spiritual growth and service.

In this book you will read stories of the many healings that have taken place through the clearings I facilitated. They range from people with a variety of medical and emotional issues and include seemingly miraculous events. They include clients who have released various forms of sickness and blockages in life from their bodies—to a house clearing where a young child was being terrorized by dark energies only she could see and feel to a woman trapped in an unwanted and serious federal court case after having been witness to something that put her in the position of testifying against organized crime. Forty-eight hours after working with her to clear negative energies, the federal agency involved called her and told her they would no longer need her testimony and that she was released from that responsibility.

Each client feels my energy, and I allow transformative energies to flow through me from higher dimensional beings to heal their energies and remove the darkness within them.

Further chapters will cover the process of clearing and re-connecting your DNA and give you an idea of how to accomplish this for yourself. At the end of each chapter will be a short exercise and meditation for you to prepare yourself. Each one builds up to the next, so I encourage you to read from beginning to end and follow the roadmap set out for you.

I ask you to begin now.

Exercise:

If you want to be the magnificent being the Divine Creator intended you to be, you must first learn to listen to your heart instead of your head. For in your heart are the answers you are so desperately searching for at this time. We are all different pieces of the Divine Creator.

Sit in an upright position, your feet flat on the floor. Relax your body.

As you begin to breathe in and out, visualize that your breath is coming into and out of your heart.

Breathe deeply this way slowly and easily three times.

Shift your thinking from your head to your heart. Go deep within your heart.

Sit quietly and listen as your heart speaks to you. What do you hear?

If you find yourself having an emotional response, know that you are releasing many years of heartache and pain. As you wander through the heart to the other side of pain you will find your authentic self.

There you will want to sit and be with all that you are. This is where you build your strength. Just as the butterfly bursts forth from the transformative cocoon, you must build strength in your authentic self to come forth.

Affirmation:

I am open and ready to listen to the feeling voice of my heart. My heart knows and only wants the very best for me.

I am ready and willing to open my soul to my divine mission.

CHAPTER TWO

The universe is transformation;
our life is what our thoughts make it.
Marcus Aurelius

Living Between Worlds

———————— ▬ ————————

We live in extraordinary times. Do you ever have the feeling that what you are experiencing is not "real"? That what you perceive through your five senses is apparent, but just does not have a sense of reality about it? You are walking between the third and fourth dimensions of consciousness.

Who Do You Think You Are?

Take a look in the mirror. What do you see? If you looked *really* closely you could see approximately fifty trillion cells working in perfect harmony to make up your physical body—skin cells, eye cells, hair cells, liver cells, pancreas cells, brain cells, toenail cells. Most likely that is not the first vision that comes to mind when you look in the mirror, but that is a reality. When you come right down to it, the reflection in the mirror is not a true picture either—it is the reverse of you, the perspective others have when they look at you.

Each cell has atoms composed of neutrons and protons which are in motion—in other words, vibrating. In other words, YOU are in continual motion. YOU vibrate. The only reason that you see yourself the way you do—in your third-dimensional reality—and the world around you that is also in motion is because your senses—sight, hearing, touch, taste, smell—perceive it that way. But what those senses are actually doing is translating *vibration*. However, even the table in front of you or the couch you sit upon is composed of energy that vibrates. It is denser than you are, and so their neutrons and protons vibrate *very* slowly.

The basic truth is that we are made of energy, and we *are* energy. Quantum physics tells us at the innermost level we come from a massive Field of energy from which everything emerges and everything returns. This Field is referred to as "Zero Point Energy" but some scientists even refer to The Field as the "Mind of God."

We know that energy can neither be created nor destroyed. Energy can only be transformed. Sort of like water when it transmutes to steam or to ice then back to water. It is a fact that energy vibrates. How do we transform energy from one form into another? We create through thought, emotion, and action. But everything, EVERYTHING is thought first.

You know this is true. You can sense energy. Ever felt the energy in a church? Or in a hospital?

Have you felt the anticipation and joy at a wedding? The grief and/or sadness at a funeral? What is the difference you feel when you walk into a cemetery, a school, or a mall? First, your Right Brain senses/feels what is going on, and then your Left Brain thinks about it and attempts to translate it. But you sense the vibration first because you pick up on the frequency of the group energy. Ever been in an environment where your immediate reaction was discomfort but you could not ascertain any reason for feeling that way? That is because you sense first and then think about it and recognize it.

So, if you wish to change your life, you must begin by changing your thought. Change your thought and you create something new. So it stands to reason that in order to change our vibration, we do it by way of everything we think, everything we feel, everything we say and do.

Thoughts are electrical; emotions are magnetic. So the way in which we emit that energy—the way in which our energy vibrates—attracts people and experiences that are resonating on the same frequency. Like attracts like. When we are in a state of vibrational balance and vital peace, we will attract to ourselves more of the same. When we are out of balance, when we are in anger, hatred, despair, we emit that vibration as well, and those people and experiences are attracted into our experience that are on that "wavelength."

Which would you rather have? Of course it is not absolute, and there is a wide spectrum of frequencies in the scale between love and hate, for example. At some point you feel more hatred than love, and at another point you feel more love than hatred. It is your choice, your thought, and your emotion that moves you up and down that scale.

Let us begin with who you *think* you are. It is with every thought you have that you create your existence. When you think about yourself, what words do you use to describe yourself? Think about it now. What words pop into your brain? Write them down. Did you write down Powerful, Unlimited, Abundant, or Loving? Able to leap tall buildings in a single bound?

Maybe. Maybe not.

By now you must have read or heard the famous quote by Pierre Teilhard de Chardin: "We are not human beings having a spiritual experience. We are spiritual beings having a human experience." Spiritual. What does that mean to you? Does that conjure up rules and regulations for you? Do you say, "Well, if I do what I'm supposed to do then I can attain everlasting heaven—but only if I can follow those rules." I have no argument or judgment about the rules or codes of conduct in any religion. You merely have to ask yourself, "How do the rules make me *feel*?" Am I in alignment with these rules?

The codes of conduct about love, kindness, and joy are particularly nice and usually make us feel pretty good. Every great religion has those. There are others that don't feel quite so good—the ones about judgment, retribution, and hellfire—but you may feel obligated to follow them in order to be a full-fledged member of your particular religious community or for your own belief system to allow you to experience heaven.

I encourage you to shift your thinking into that which you really are. And who is that? Only you know.

At the very simplest level let us take the example of fixing dinner. The thought occurs to you that you have to make a dinner for yourself or your family this evening. What are you going to do? Well, your brain then goes off to the races. What sounds good? What do I like to eat? What does my family like? What do I want? What do I like to cook? What do I have in stock in order to make what I want? Do I need to make a trip to the store for a missing ingredient?

And then you are off and onto the work of preparing the dinner, thus creating the dinner, cooking the dinner, serving the dinner, eating the dinner. But it all began with thought.

Then the next step is how you *feel*. Sometimes mere semantics can shift your thinking. If you tell yourself that feeding your family is a burdensome job you *have* to do, you hate it and it is an issue for you. It becomes all those feelings, and cooking dinner is anything but a joyous experience for you. But if you can tell yourself that you are fortunate because you *get* to cook dinner for your family and how pleased you are when they appreciate the food you have prepared and move down the pathway of that thinking, your feeling will shift about what you do, and eventually it will become a joyous experience for you.

So it is with every thing in your life. It all begins with a thought. No matter how simple or complex. Higher mathematics came about because someone began to think about it. Medications were created because someone began to think and experiment and think some more and then "discovered" the answer. The mystery novel you might love to read was first an idea in the mind of the writer before a word was put on a page.

Do you ever *feel* about what you think? How do you *feel* about all of that? How often do you consider your feelings about what you are creating through thought?

That is where the power comes in. A thought is just a thought. It has no power of its own. You have millions of them every day. They flit in and out. Some of them you give your attention to, others you let drift. The ones that you give power to are the ones that you add feeling to such as the following:

"What am I going to do about that child?"

"Why won't my husband/wife do 'x'?"

"I love my work."

"I hate my work."

"I am afraid."

"I am lonely."

"I am happy."

"My car broke down again."

"I have no money."

"I have so much money."

How do you create from your thinking? We easily see the sequence when we think about our intention to cook dinner. However, it is not so apparent when we think about abundance, health, or finding a mate. We believe those things are different. They really are no different from preparing dinner. We just have convinced ourselves through our belief system that they are. In "reality" they are illusions that we have created and imbued belief into them and so made them "real."

It does not matter if you believe me or not. Ask yourself if you *feel* change is coming. The answer I am sure is, yes, change is coming. On some level you do feel it. Change is inevitable. It is what expands the Universe and takes it to places no one has ever been before. It is unbelievably significant. If we do not change, we die because the life force that propels change comes to an end.

If you could step back (way back) and look at the world, what would be the patterns you would see? Unrest, discomfort, dis-ease, restlessness, upheaval. What are these signs of? New birth. We are birthing the next age. As with any birth it is hard to see the wonders of the outcome when all we are experiencing is the pain and suffering of that birth. But what mother does not willingly participate in the experience so that she may birth a beloved child? What child does not immediately bond with love to the mother that lovingly births it?

That is our future, but it is hard to see it now because we participate in a three-dimensional reality and as far as we can remember, always have.

Right now you are in between two worlds. The world that is—the third-dimensional world that has seemed so solid and so secure—and the fifth-dimensional world—that will shortly be upon us. This will be a world based on love. This will be a world where you will be at one (at-one-ment) with your Higher Self/God/the All and the All that is you. You will *know* and can have access to the information and wisdom that resides in all the dimensions. There will be no separation. You will vibrate at a higher level of consciousness than you can imagine right now and live in a world where the rational mind has given way to the intuitive, feeling mind.

Can you feel that on any level? Do you feel the restlessness of that? Does it resonate with you on any level? As difficult as it is to accept with your Left Brain, is your Right Brain screaming YES? If so that is the real reason you picked up this book and the person next to you—who may be your dearest friend—just rolled his or her eyes.

It is time for us to evolve. Are you, will you, be ready for that evolution?

Who Are You Really?

The first step on the road to preparation is the discovery of who and what you are. You have incredible power at your disposal. This power comes not from outside of you, but from within yourself. That power is not given to you. You already own it. How many times have you been told that we humans are created in the very image of God? If God if everywhere and in everything, then God is in us. Who we really are is God. (Recall the Teilhard de Chardin quote from above?)

You may have been told that the physical you is all that is. If this book called to you, then you know that is not true to you. You do not believe that. You know you are more.

The truth is, the physical is only a minor part, a small part of who you are. There is a larger part, a huge part—the nonphysical, Soul/Expanded You/ Higher You, whatever semantics you feel comfortable to describe It—that exists on a whole other level. That part of you adores you, loves you unconditionally, and sees you as nothing less than the magnificent being you already are.

So if you are so powerful, so magnificent, why not choose what you think and therefore create your existence? That must mean that you are pretty powerful in order to be able do that. When you were born, you lost consciousness of who you truly are. Once in the physical you had to rebuild. From the non-physical perspective, this was going to be fun—going to be a game, the purpose of which was joy. Can you imagine how anything could be more fun for highly developed beings than to forget everything they know, throw themselves into the maze of life on planet Earth, and then figure it back out? Whoo hoo! What an adventure, what a ride! Well, it is time to remember, to wake up to that which you are—a powerful, magnificent being of light—and get on with enjoying the ride.

So that must mean that you are not broken, you are whole. That must mean that you can no longer believe you cannot because *you can*. It must mean that you are no longer alone; you have the ever-present nonphysical, Soul/Expanded You/ Higher You to see you through *anything*.

A Woman With Legal Problems

One day a woman called me desperate for a solution to a problem she had. She was literally at her wit's end and did not know where else to turn. She told me that the she had taken a position working for a company that created a financial product that turned out to be fraudulent. She had no idea that the company was involved in any criminal activities until she was well entrenched in her position.

The FBI had gotten involved and was going to prosecute the company, hoping that it would lead them to the real organizers, and they insisted they needed her help to do it. She had a child, and when she called me she had already received several death threats. This had been going on for some time and she was consumed with worry. She began drinking to ease the pain. She came to me on a Wednesday, and the following Monday she was supposed to fly to Miami and testify in federal court.

It was apparent to me that she had a soul filled with light. Using my regular procedure, I cleared all the negative energies around her and sealed off any portals that were open to keep those energies from returning. Then I asked her if anyone had prayed for the prosecution. Of course, when you are involved in any adversarial situation, you rarely think of the opposing side or their issues. After her session, we spent some time praying for harmony and smoothness and that everything would work out for the highest and best of all involved.

That night she attended a group meeting for support. After the meeting, she e-mailed me that the woman who'd sat next to her had exclaimed, "I am so privileged to sit by you. Your energy is wonderful!"

The next day, on Thursday afternoon, the FBI called her to tell her that they had cancelled her plane reservations because she no longer needed to testify. She had two legal issues—one with her old company who was suing her—and the other involved her testimony in federal court. Once she didn't have to testify, the company dropped the charges against her. Her reality was *shifted*.

You are powerful. You are unlimited. It is you who limit yourself by saying and believing that you are not for whatever reason. The truth is there are no excuses. There is only energy. That energy vibrates and it attracts—what you want and what you do not want.

Movement from Unconscious to Conscious

Once you realize this, *know* this, you go from an unconscious state of being to one of consciousness. You are aware of being aware of who you really are. Because of the state of the world today in the third dimension and the angst going on, you are being shaken awake instead of gradually coming to it through study, experience, or practice. You must know in your very bones that there *has* to be more than *this*! Regardless of how you came to consciousness, there is no going back to unconsciousness. And you may be experiencing some discomfort. "So, I'm conscious," you say. "So there's no going back. Now what do I do?"

Anything you want. Consciousness, the combination of you and your ever-present nonphysical, Soul/Expanded You/ Higher You create your world. Currently that world is three-dimensional— it has width, breadth, and height. You can touch, taste, smell, feel, see, and hear it. But that is going to change soon.

What you looked upon formerly as separate soon will be perceived in relation to, in connection to, the whole. We are all interdependent. This new consciousness will exist in the hearts of all people. It will include wisdom, purity, compassion, and, most importantly, love in our daily lives. Later on we will ask, "When love is the only currency, how rich will you be?" But you might want to start thinking about it right now.

Your Work is Internal

As I stated before, who you are is who you think you are. Start with loving yourself. Love your body, but love that which you *are*—the part of you created in divine image. The Master, Jesus Christ, made the point that the most important commandment was to love God and love your neighbor as yourself. We easily skip over the intermediate step inherent in what he said—that you must first love self before it is possible to love your neighbor. The easiest way to begin to do this is with powerful self-talk.

Look at your self in the mirror; *smile* at yourself. Do this every day. Gradually move on to all the other positive aspects you know about yourself. If this is difficult for you, start with the small stuff. Love the part of you, you already love—the color of your hair, your skin, the shape of your toes. Love the part of you that is kind to animals, old people, and children. Love the part of you that opens doors for strangers, brings food to friends at times of sorrow, or listens to loved ones without judgment. Love the part of you that does a good job at work. Start there and appreciate those parts of you that you like the best. Build yourself up while you look in the mirror—this is a powerful exercise that helps to let go of negative self-talk.

If this is not so difficult for you, expand from where you are, increase the amount of love you flow to yourself, and then send it out to those people, places, and things that you can appreciate the most. Then send it out to those people, places, and things that you appreciate the least.

The truth is you are no good for anyone else until you are good to yourself and appreciate yourself for the truly wonderful being you are.

The Dimensions of Consciousness

Dimensions have to do with consciousness. There are many levels or strata of consciousness. Where you fit, how you proceed, is dependent upon your vibration and your consciousness.

The Third Dimension

We accept that the third dimension in which we live has width, height, and breadth. Things are dense and solid, and we perceive that density through our five senses. This is our world of form.

We also accept that there is a specific (scientific) set of rules that operates in this dimension.

However, in terms of consciousness, the third dimension—which we know and accept—is very rigid. It is based on rules and codes that encompass duality. In the third dimension, people do not live from the center of joy; they live from the center of fear. The third dimension is fear-based. That fear base comes right out of their thinking of duality.

There is right and wrong, good and bad, and people feel they *must* be right and they *must* be good. Everything is black and white. It becomes very frustrating because everything is *not* black and white. But because of the imprints and patterns that have been imposed upon us genetically, and from just living a lifetime in a lot of dysfunctional families, we are brought up thinking that we have to be this way. In the third dimension, we are our own worst enemy. We are unsure of our future; we do not trust ourselves or believe that we have any power.

In the third dimension, we think of everything, and I mean everything, as being on a scale with the most negative aspect of whatever the subject or topic is at the bottom and the most positive aspect at the top. How many times have we taken surveys in this third-dimensional reality that ask us to judge—on a scale of 1 to 10, 1 being no help at all and 10 being extremely helpful—how we felt we were served at a particular restaurant? *Everything* is conditional.

You live in a reactive state of mind. It is natural for you to react to the conditions around you. When something happens to you or around you, your response is a natural outcome of your conditioned reactions. Oftentimes we refer to these as "knee-jerk reactions". In other words, you feel you have no choice, you just respond. For example, when someone is rude to you, you have no other choice but to be rude back. This is a basic understanding of road rage and it is easy to see how it escalates. The truth of the matter is there are always other ways to respond, we just have not conditioned ourselves to see them because we live in a world of duality – right/wrong, black/white, good/evil.

This concept is very similar to the one in Eckhart Tolle's book *A New Earth*. In it he refers to the "pain bodies." In the third dimension there are a lot of pain bodies.

Part of stepping out of the third dimension is learning that we have the power to remove the pain bodies, to let them go. Feeling powerless, feeling as if we are a victim of circumstances, is a big part of being in the third dimension. When I work with clients and check their Chakra Energy Centers, I often discover low energy in the solar plexus which represents personal power. To heal this Chakra and allow full power is part of my prayer for healing personal pain.

The second aspect of the third dimension is time. We accept that time moves in a straight line, in one direction. We understand past, present, and future. We constantly mull over our past and spend our present preparing for the future. We constantly look to what is in front of us or what is behind us. We believe that those who ignore history are doomed to repeat it. So we spend a lot of time analyzing history, afraid of making the same mistakes over and over again.

The left brain, the rational mind, rules in the third dimension. Everything is based on analyzing a situation, making lists, controlling, storing information, making decisions based on information we collect. We calculate, we synthesize, and we draw conclusions from those conditions that we observe.

Move on to connecting and being with a higher Divine being through meditation and going within yourself. The only way to discover the answers is inside yourself. We end up looking for everything on the outside—how people are reacting to us. How much love am I bringing to myself? If I do "that" will they love me more?

What we have to realize so that we can step into the fourth dimension is that love is unconditional. How often do you think, "God must love that person more because they make more money than I do and they are more successful?" That is only true because you think it is. You have to turn your head around and start re-thinking and re-feeling the concept of unconditional love.

Part of my healing work is removing chaos in the mind of thoughts of the past and future and what the person should do now. These are thoughts which include the words I could, I should, what if, I had better do this or that, or have to, got to. Change your words and live in choice. These thoughts block you from your power—the power of living in your now moment. The only time that exists is now. You only have now in which to create.

The third dimension is filled with struggle. It is natural for us to feel that the proper thing to do is the thing that we "should" do. We often are hard on ourselves because we "should have" done this or that. It is time for us to stop "shoulding" on ourselves.

Once we start—one step at a time—letting go of struggle, whether it is finding the perfect partner or the perfect job, finding the money we deserve, finding the perfect place to live, we begin to recognize all that is ours already and we are no longer just surrendering or allowing these things to come to us.

Once we allow those things to come to us, our consciousness will increase. There is no choice in the third dimension because we don't feel we are in control. We all have choices—realize you always live in the power of your choice. Change how you speak to yourself in choice. Positive words of choice increase the flow of energy.

Let go of the struggle and the feeling that you have to pull whatever it is to you. It is not a matter of reaching out and finding it and *making* it come to you. It is a matter of opening up your magnetic energy fields to a higher vibration. When that vibration comes in contact with one who can feel that and know that and recognize that, it will come to you. Remember, all we are is energy. That energy vibrates, and how we feel creates a magnetic pulse that pulls what we want to us. We just show up as a physical being because *our senses translate vibration into the density of a physical form.*

How do you master the third dimension? By realizing, by becoming conscious, that it is all an *illusion.* Living in the third dimension is an illusion because everything you think and feel you made up. Fear is the best example of that. You make fear up—it does not exist until you create it in whatever situation you allow it to exist for you. Let go of these illusions. Let go of the struggle.

It begins with self-talk. You must be cognizant of what you say to yourself, in your mind about what you are thinking and feeling.

I had a friend once who said, "I wouldn't have any luck at all if I didn't have bad luck." What a debilitating thought and what a self-fulfilling prophecy!

We are not alone in the Universe. The third dimension is a drag on the entire Universe. Since we are all one, we keep everyone back when we cling to this consciousness due to its density. Therefore, it depends on us in this consciousness evolutionary process to move forward, release fear, and live in unconditional love and choice in order to move forward.

The Fourth Dimension

The fourth dimension is the pathway through the forest out of the physical and into the divine part of your consciousness. You must travel this pathway in order to be able to sustain the energy that higher frequencies require.

Part of my work is to help you to wake up—to recognize that you are not tied to the third dimension. It is all right to let go of the fear, the duality, and go within instead. You must start to fully love yourself. You must start to trust who you are. Then you will begin to recognize who you are. Once again, this is the value of doing the daily "mirror talk."

A Husband Stuck in the Third Dimension

One day a client called me in tears. Since her session with me, she had been experiencing a terrible time with her husband. She loved him, but he was stuck in third-dimensional thinking.

She pleaded with me, "I have expanded, finding bliss. It just doesn't feel good to be with him anymore. Can you help him?"

After analyzing his energy fields, it was apparent that he was a Lightworker also. There are no accidents, and these two were truly meant to be with each other. Together, we called in his Higher Self to get permission to clear his energy fields so that he could feel alignment with his wife. Sometimes partnerships can work out and they can grow together. Other times a partnership may end when one feels the need to go a separate way for the highest good of all concerned. In this case, the marriage blossomed after clearing. They are growing together in the acceptance of fourth dimension consciousness, but it doesn't always work that way.

Moving into the Fourth Dimension

As you move into the fourth dimension, your awareness increases; your care and love of self increases. You *want* to take good care of yourself, you *want* to eat right, and you *want* to rest. You do not want to be in an abusive relationship. Once you start to move into the fourth dimension, you start letting go of people whom you no longer want to be around—people who just do not feel good to be around.

This is a time where you might start letting go of jobs, other people, friends and acquaintances who just don't feel good to you. You cannot fill your closet with new things if your closet is filled to capacity with the old. You must let go and surrender the old to make room for the new. It is about attracting to you what you want since once you get into fourth-dimension consciousness, you learn to attract and attract more quickly. In *Ask and It Is Given*, Jerry and Esther Hicks point out that you create a vacuum for your good to come to you when you clear out space for it. You become open to receive more and better. You can create a vacuum in your desires or energies as well.

You do not deserve to be in an abusive relationship on any level. I vividly remember the day I had a particular conversation with my mother. I tried to please her all of my life and the thought came to me one day that I was not the one to make her happy; it had to come from her own self. She made a choice to be a victim.

She would often say, "God will not give us more than we can handle," thus relegating responsibility to God for her life instead of to herself.

Even as an adult, the legacy of being the oldest of five propelled me to try and please her and make her happy. I had to recognize that I had to let go of the pain I had allowed my mother to bestow upon me—the feeling that I was never good enough to make her happy. It was time to recognize that it was one more step into the third dimension that I no longer wanted. I could choose to feel differently about it. I had to let it go—it was her life, not mine. I couldn't make her see how to live out of the third dimension. I have performed every kind of clearing I know how to do for her. She is where she is, and I accept that now without judgment. She is on her own path.

When I took that step, when I stopped calling her so often, she asked me why I didn't call her as much any more. I was very honest and said, "When I speak with you, Mother, it is not very uplifting for me."

Now when I do talk to her, she tries to be more positive because I showed her how she was coming across. Though I want her love and attention, I will not allow myself to be victimized by her need to complain to someone. She likes the third dimension; it is ingrained in her and is comfortable there. It is not where I want to be, but it is where she is.

You probably already have friends who challenge you in the same way. They may call you—and they are wonderful people—but they will tell you about their terrible husband and how they count the years until they can leave this man. Transform it. Whatever is around you is what you thought, what you created. Whatever you have in your life is what you brought to yourself. Once you recognize that the power is within you, once you tune into that power, the power that you get to *choose how you feel*, you can transition to a higher state of consciousness.

As you let go of the third dimension and step into the fourth, occasionally you will slip backward. All you have to do is recognize what it is and let it go.

As you move into the fourth dimension, things change. It is more flexible in the fourth dimension.

First of all, you realize that duality has fallen away. Things are not so hard and fast. *You have choice.* A friend of mine described this as "the third option." There is always a third option based on choice. Life in the fourth dimension is about that choice, so if you want to be there, always look for the third option.

Understand that you can choose to feel differently. You no longer have to react to conditions. Just as I made a choice about how I was going to feel about my mother. You can observe the conditions and decide how you feel about them. There is an alignment that comes into play which balances out those opposing forces. It is what feels better and what is best for all. Things no longer appear to be so bad or so good, so right or so wrong.

Secondly, only the present exists. You begin to live in the now moment. The present is your point of power as it is in the present moment that you create. Today is all that matters. Perhaps some of you who read this recognize that on some level you have already moved into one of the strata of the fourth dimension based upon this feeling about time in your life. There is no past. There is no future. There is only the now moment, the most important moment in your life.

Third, since things are unconditional they therefore encompass choice. You no longer have to react to the conditions of any situation. You can choose consciously to initiate something else in any moment. You can *choose* to feel something different. External events, situations, communications no longer have the power over you because **you no longer react to them in a knee-jerk fashion**.

Now in the previous example above on the rating scale, you may *choose* to give the server the benefit of the doubt—perhaps he or she had a bad day or was new to the job or perhaps just needed encouragement. You are beginning to let go of the rational and depend on the intuitive side of your brain. What you thought a moment ago about the server—that he was just a bad server—is no longer true. You have a new reality based on what you choose to believe and feel is true.

In the fourth dimension you can start manifesting more easily. Visualizing, knowing something is yours and allowing it to come to you becomes simpler. Ideas just pop up. Once you step from the fourth dimension to the fifth, it is like magic every day of your life.

How does one master the fourth dimension? Through the use of your Higher Mind. In your Higher Mind ask yourself: "Is this of love or is it the fear that love is not present?" If you can see that everything is love, then you will begin to understand that there is no separation. If you can release judgment and see things through the eyes of the Source of All—who you are in physical form—then you will be transformed.

Transformation takes place when you can stand at the doorway of any event—tragedy, crisis, war, etc., and see it through those eyes. The more you consciously choose, the easier it gets, and eventually it is automatic. You will not want to live any other way but from the heart of who you are, in choice.

Use Your Higher Mind

There is a place in your brain in which resides the pineal gland. It is located in the geometric center of your skull. Oftentimes this space is referred to as the Third Eye or the Inner Vision. From a physiological standpoint, the pineal gland is a photosensitive organ that acts as an important timekeeper for the body. It works in conjunction with the hypothalamus gland that regulates thirst, hunger, sexual desire, and our aging process.

However, for centuries, mystical tradition held that this area in the middle of the brain is the link between the physical and spiritual worlds. It has always been important in opening up to the development of psychic abilities, for awareness of the "sixth sense." If you are awakening to these abilities, you may feel a pressure at the base of the brain. Sometimes these abilities are awakened through a head injury, thus the many stories of people who have suddenly acquired visionary abilities after an accident.

In any case, if you think of this area in your brain as your Higher Mind, you can deliberately place focus there. You can begin to develop abilities to see beyond the physical to the metaphysical if you can start to "see" through the Higher Mind and through the feeling heart.

This is the way you can tap into a connection with your Higher Self and with the Archangels, Ascended Masters, and other Beings of Light who are available to you to assist and help you on your journey.

There is a pure Soul within all beings. You might not see it at first within yourself or others, but if you can begin to look through your Higher Mind, you will begin to see that which exists within yourself and others. If you can view the world and everything in it as a place where even the smallest detail of your day can truly be *appreciated*, your life will change dramatically and you will start to move between and among the dimensions of consciousness.

Know that the Divine Creator loves you and only wants the very best for you. Therefore, love yourself; know the very best is here. *You just cannot see it yet.* Know that instead of thinking that you will believe it when you see it, it is the very act of believing (or faith) that causes the physical manifestation. In other words believe first and then you will see it. These are very helpful words to use in your self-talk when you cannot see a way out of a situation or you have no idea what to do next.

In my sessions with clients I ask for full activation and healing of the pineal gland which opens the doorway to becoming more telepathic and intuitive.

As a daily practice, attempt to set up a way to feel an emotion and not feel bad about it or good about it but just recognize that you are feeling it. Disengage from the event that brought on the emotion and tune into how you feel about it.

The Fifth Dimension

The fifth dimension is one of Light and Love in which we are able to manifest our desires. It is "magic" and encompasses amazing realizations of synchronicity.

The fifth dimension is where you want to be. It is where we are *all* headed. It is the place where Heaven exists on Earth. Earth is Heaven when it is fueled by love and compassion and the sense of being one with all. In this dimension of consciousness you will accept the individual rights of each living being while at the same time have the ability to see that everything is interdependent and synchronistic.

When you attain fifth-dimensional consciousness, you experience a reintegration with your Soul/ Expanded You/ Higher Self. You become one with the realm of the Spiritual. There is no longer a sense of separation from you and You. It brings with it higher awareness and allows you to know yourself at the Soul level. You are who you came here to *be*. You vibrate at a higher level, a higher frequency than you ever thought possible. Your highest desire is to somehow be of service in the best sense of the word. Finding your mission of service is bliss.

Thought is reality because in the fifth dimension simultaneous time exists. You think it, and it manifests into the world of form. Therefore, it is essential that you master your thoughts and emotions before entering this level of consciousness. Leave your past behind you. It needs to be transmuted by positive thoughts, and if we can do that, then life will really soar on this planet.

The right brain rules the fifth dimension. You think and feel from your heart. You are connected to your Higher Self and your heart. Your innate spiritual abilities increase and reveal themselves. These include all the abilities we currently attribute only to those "gifted" with abilities such as clairvoyance, telepathy, and intuition. You are fully and completely conscious.

What 2012 Brings

The third dimension is held together, weighed down if you will, by the dense magnetic field that covers the planet. That field is breaking up. Scientists have already become concerned because they are aware that the magnetic field of the earth is dissolving. As of this writing, a huge hole in the earth's magnetic field has been discovered and noted. Some scientists are already concerned about the size of the solar storms slated for

2012 that will occur right on time in their scientifically predicted eleven-year cycle.

Because of the break-up of the earth's magnetic field, the "shields are down." The shields being what normally protect us from these solar storms. Already scientists are trying to warn governments and companies of the possibility of vast power outages, the reality of satellites not working, and the fact that communications as we know it may be knocked out all over the earth. They are urging those same governments and companies to cooperate and "prepare" for what will shortly be upon us.

What the decrease in the density of earth's magnetic field means on a spiritual level is that it will create a cleansing that will allow us to access our Higher Selves, to raise our vibration and transmute into the fifth dimension.

In addition, you may not be aware that the earthquake in Haiti in the spring of 2010 caused a very slight shift in the axis of the earth. It set time off by one millionth of one second. We are beginning to let go of the denser nature of the third dimension and experience the beginnings of the shift that will occur in 2012.

None of this is meant to create fear in those who read it. That would be an attempt to trap you into staying in the third dimension. It is merely mentioned to make you more aware of what is happening, how we are evolving along with the new earth, and to prepare you to think and feel differently so that you too may evolve in consciousness.

Exercise:

Begin a program of "mirror work."

I do this on a regular basis, and it is very transformative. Once I started, I quickly found a big increase in confidence and joy that resulted in feeling very good about myself.

Look at yourself in the mirror at least twice a day:

1. Look deeply into your beautiful eyes.

2. Think of all the things you appreciate in your life—say them out loud.

3. Be outrageous with your self-talk. What would you really like to hear someone say about you? Say that to yourself and mean it.

This is very powerful; do it often—especially when you see a big beautiful mirror!

Exercise:

Keep a pen or pencil and a pad of paper by your bed.

When you wake up and before you get up, give yourself some self-talk about your perfect life.

1. What do you expect to find in your Heaven on Earth?

2. Write it out when you think of it.

3. Keep adding to the list.

Affirmations:

I thank the Divine Creator for the divine synchronicities in my life today.

I find joy and love everywhere I go and in every thing I do.

Today and every day I am living in my Heaven on Earth.

CHAPTER THREE

Love is life. All, everything that I understand, I understand only because I love. Everything is, everything exists, only because I love. Everything is united by it alone. Love is God, and to die means that I, a particle of love, shall return to the general and eternal source.

Leo Tolstoy

You Are Not Alone

——————— ■ ———————

Information about our innate power to create what we want and who we truly are has always been available to those who search for it. Mystery schools over the ages were established for just this reason but their initiates were instructed to keep the secret. Still, there were books such as *The Master Key* by Charles Haanel, *The Science of Getting Rich* by Wallace D. Wattles, *The Kybalion* by Three Initiates, and the familiar *Think and Grow Rich* by Napoleon Hill which all revealed parts of the truth.

In the last century, the first real wave of information available to us came from those who had awakened and moved into higher consciousness. From a spiritual sense it can be said to have begun with the Harmonic Convergence in 1987. Tony Shearer wrote a book in 1971 entitled *Quetzalcoatl*

Lord of the Dawn which based its dates on the Mayan Calendar. It was also researched by Dr. Jose Arguellas, and he was the stimulus for the convocation of people in 1987 to meet at sacred sites all over the world to celebrate what many saw as the beginning of the countdown to December 21, 2012, when the long-cycle Mayan Calendar ends. This was the first wave of information sent out into the world about the Shift in consciousness. Those involved numbered in the tens of thousands worldwide.

The second wave took place during the 1990s. More books started to be published by alternative publishing companies, and authors began to emerge. Since that time there has been a plethora of books covering every topic from extraterrestrials to Ascension and the fifth dimension. They are written from every viewpoint from that of a higher being "channeled" by the author to that which has been scientifically discovered and "verified." Many seminars took place to teach those interested in finding out more. All the information focused on what was going to take place over the course of the next twenty years. Those involved numbered several million.

In 2000, the third wave took place which included even more books and seminars on more and more topics in harmony with the coming Shift. Those involved now number well over fifty million. In a world of six billion people, this is still less than one percent of the population.

At the writing of this book we are less than two years away from 2012, and the Internet abounds with more information than one person could possibly assimilate in the time remaining. How many millions are involved now and where is the percentage of the population preparing for what is about to happen?

If you think you are alone or somehow "strange" because you think many of the things outlined in this book make sense to you on some level, know that you are not alone. Most likely you have researched or come into contact with other books or readings like it. Know that every day others like you are feeling the same pull toward this knowledge. Time is speeding up, more and more people are awakening and becoming conscious of the spiritual shift that is about to occur and accepting and working within their own lives to move to higher consciousness. You are not alone.

Critical Mass

There is a theory called the "hundredth monkey theory." It refers to a species of monkey on an isolated island that learned a new behavior. Researchers observed a few of the monkeys begin to wash sand off of potatoes before eating them. Eventually, other monkeys copied this behavior. Suddenly and simultaneously monkeys of the same species on nearby islands also began to wash their potatoes in the same manner; then this species of monkeys exhibited this behavior all over the world. This is also the basis of the "tipping point" which can be defined as the point at which momentum for change becomes inevitable. It is sensed energetically and then translated into action and/or understanding.

Eventually the world will hit a point of critical mass in terms of accepting that as a species and a planet we are moving toward life in the fifth dimension. This book is part of that movement. It is my intention to help as many people as I can prepare for what is going to happen by the end of 2012. I invite you to awaken with the rest of us and move into that place of love so that we can *all* move easily into the years that will follow.

We think we are all alone on the planet. We think the only reality is the one that exists in the third dimension. Because we are energy beings, we are all connected. In truth there are many dimensions, many universes right in the room in which you sit and read this book. Quantum physics tells us that what we consider our reality is only the observer effect. All possibilities exist, but the one that we give our attention to, *the one we focus upon, is the one that exists for us.*

Lightworkers

There are many Lightworkers who are attracted to New Age and metaphysical books. They are continually searching for answers; they are non-conformist. There is probably at least one in your own family. Most likely it is you! Oftentimes, your friends and family come to you to seek answers to the questions that impact their lives—not the what, but the why of some event or circumstance. You may be considered the "changeling" in the family but you know, on an intuitive level, the answers to their questions.

A Lightworker is a person who feels there is a definite purpose for being here now. You may find yourself searching for that purpose or mission above all other things.

A Lightworker is a person who welcomes the Light and consciously holds it for others to see in order to assist them in re-membering who they truly are. Lightworkers all over the world are at work to prepare for the coming times ahead.

There are many Lightworkers on the planet at this time. It is easy to find them on the Internet and in your community. So many are working to help bring the changes to the planet in as easy a way as possible. Because you are reading this book, you may be a Lightworker or were led here by someone who is.

As a civilization, we have gotten to the point where we can no longer afford to believe we are alone in the universe—in the many universes. Even statistics will support the fact that in the multitude of galaxies that exist there has to be other planets that have capability for life as we know it. Why couldn't they have life as we *do not know it*, but sense it? As the Source of All is unlimited, why would the creations of that Source be limited? Some aspects of the media, movies, and books prepare us for First Contact with other beings from other dimensions and worlds. However, how they make that look is pure Hollywood.

Because other dimensions exist, it makes sense that there are beings that exist on those other dimensions as well. While it may be true that these civilizations are more technologically advanced than we are, it stands to reason that many must be more spiritually evolved than we are as well. Each one of us, as well as each one of them, owes their own evolution to those who are more advanced. The Source of All created all of these worlds, and all life. So it stands to reason that there are other Lightworkers on other planets and dimensions who are ready to help us as well. Many are standing nearby wanting to help, but cannot intervene unless asked. If there is a Prime Directive—as in the Star Trek Tradition—it has to be that we all have freewill. If we want help, *we just have to ask.*

Angels and Ascended Masters

Angels are accepted in almost every culture across the world. Their mission is to protect, nurture, and guide us. In the Bible, Angels often act as messengers of God. They often assist in times of change—and certainly the period we are going through now and through 2012 qualify for that definition. Angels radiate the unconditional love of the Source of All and can assist us to do the same. As we are a universe of freewill, we must ask for their assistance first.

The Archangel Michael's special task is to work with Lightworkers on the planet today. He is the only angel recognized by name in Judaism, Christianity, and Islam. A powerful Being of Light, he is present to assist in the transformation of the planet in the next few years. If you feel drawn to him, it is another sign in discovering the true purpose of your mission as a Lightworker.

There are Beings of Light on other realms that stand ready and willing assist in bringing more light to planet Earth. Your spiritual guides also stand ready to help when called upon as well as the Ascended Masters. The Ascended Masters are those who have had earthly incarnations and showed the way for the rest of us. They have conquered death and progressed so high on the spiritual ladder that there is no longer any need for them to incarnate in the physical.

If you are interested in finding out what Archangels and Ascended Masters you would like to invite into your life and/or ask for assistance, I highly recommend Doreen Virtue's book *Archangels & Ascended Masters: A Guide to Working and Healing with Divinities and Deities.*

There is a caveat in place here. These are non-physical beings that you may ask for assistance and guidance. You are physical. That means that they can send people, ideas, events, opportunities your way—but you have to take advantage of them. You have to be open to receiving their guidance and then choose what feels best to you and take action. I advise you not to rest on your laurels or assume that the Being of Light whose aid you invoked is taking care of absolutely everything.

For example, I invoked the guidance and assistance of the Archangel Gabriel and the Ascended Master St. Germain in the development of this book. And I have to say I was guided and inspired to books, research, and people in interesting and unusual ways. However, I was the one that organized the ideas, created a plan, and sat at the computer keyboard on a regular schedule and typed out the manuscript. I never expected to wake up some morning and find that the some unseen hand had written the whole thing out and left a neat pile of typewritten pages my kitchen counter!

There are other beings on other planets, other civilizations in the galaxy, watching closely to see how we are doing. Once again, they are ready to give us assistance now, and we can receive it by calling out to them.

A word of caution. While most of these beings are positive in nature, there are other forces, ET's, who live on the energy of fear and limitation who do not want us to succeed in our evolution. They are another reason why it is so important for us to move up to the fifth dimension and live in love instead of fear. They are the forces of darkness, attempting to prevent or slow down the influx of Light into our world, but they will not accomplish their wish to keep the planet and us from the process of ascension.

Whenever you do call out for help, always surround yourself with the Light and Love of the Divine Creator first and ask for the highest and best to come to your aid. You will be answered.

Starseeds

Starseeds are Beings that have incarnated on earth but their *souls* originated from other places in the Universe—other planets as well as non-physical dimensions. At this time, millions of starseeds have incarnated on earth so that they may help the inhabitants as well as Mother Earth herself. These beings often are the ones gifted with the ability to heal, to channel higher dimensional beings and to offer spiritual education and information. My soul originated in Sirius, and therefore I am a Sirian starseed.

There is a major wake-up call going on for humanity right now. An example of this call has come in terms of the "green" movement. People have become aware of what pollution has been doing to our home planet and have begun to act. Ten years ago no one had even heard of the term "green." Now we see commercials about all kinds of green products. Recycling has become very popular and is done on a regular basis—all levels of society cooperate and participate in these programs.

So it will be soon with the spiritual movement—people are waking up every day to their true potential, and it is the starseeds who are leading the way and who will be looked to in the coming days for guidance and clarification.

Sirians

The Sirians have visited our planet for millennia. Sirius consists of a cluster of three stars called by our astronomers Sirius A, Sirius B, and Sirius C. This cluster makes up the brightest star in the night sky, and it is eight light years from our planet. Many Sirian starseeds are on the planet today to assist in the transition to the fifth dimension.

Patricia Cori channels the Sirian High Council, and she is author of a number of books, most notably *No More Secrets No More Lies: A Handbook to Starseed Awakening.* Her website *www.sirianrevelations.net* includes some of her channeling and has information and teachings about the coming events to 2012 and Sirian involvement in them. Her latest book *Transition Now: Redefining Duality 2012 and Beyond* came out at the time I was in the process of writing this book.

Pleiadians

The Pleiadians, like the Sirians, have a long history with the earth. Pleiadians are from a star system called Pleiades. This star system is a small cluster of seven stars located in the Constellation of Taurus the Bull; it is five hundred light years from planet Earth. Pleiadian Lightworkers are here to help raise the vibration of the planet in time for Ascension to the fifth dimension.

Barbara Marciniak channels The Pleiadians. She is the author of *Bringers of the Dawn* and many other books. Her website *www.pleiadians. com* is very helpful in understanding Pleiadian involvement in our planet at this time.

Arcturians

The Arcturians come from the fourth brightest star in our sky. Dr. Norma Milanovich, founder of the Athena Leadership Center, channels messages from Ascended Masters and has written *We, The Arcturians* which outlines the mission and assistance being offered to earth at this time. Her website *www.ourtrustisingod.com* offers insight and inspiration.

Exercise:

If it is possible for you, now is time to visit sacred centers of earth which are all over the world. Many of these places are in the United States and include the following:

Chaco Canyon, New Mexico

Devil's Tower, Wyoming

Mauna Kea and Haleakala, Hawaii

Mt. Shasta, California

Sacred Mountains of the Southwest

Sedona, Arizona

Shiprock, New Mexico

White Sands, New Mexico

In Mexico: the Sacred Mayan and Aztec sites

If it is not possible to travel at this time do so through the Internet or the exploration of books on the topics of these Sacred sites. See what resonates for you—what speaks to you emotionally. When I had the privilege to visit the Mayan temple at Chichen Itza, I had a profound spiritual experience. I know the same kind of experience is available to you at any one of the sacred sites that call to you.

Exercise:

Create an altar in your home that resonates with you and where you can find peace being there and meditating there.

Put representations of all of the four ele-ments on the altar: earth, wind, fire, and water. Add subjects that are sacred to you: statues or pictures that mean something special to you.

Affirmations:

I am a child of the Universe and all is well in my universe.

I am beloved. I am not alone.

I am assisted and defended by powerful Beings of Light; all I have to do is ask.

CHAPTER FOUR

And I will show wonders in heaven above,

and signs in the earth beneath...

Acts of the Apostles 2:19

There Are Signs All Over The Place

———————■———————

What a world we live in today! It is truly a wonderful time to be on the planet and experience this time of change as we shift from the third dimension of density into the fifth dimension of Heaven on Earth. This is the most exciting thing that has ever happened on our planet and it will happen in a very short amount of time—in our lifetime! We are here for a reason. We are the ones who have chosen to be here to greet this new consciousness and bring it forward into the light.

This is the dimension of pure love and joy that helps develop the state of oneness. For those Lightworkers searching for the answers to what is going on, now is the time to explore the many changing energies permeating earth.

Veils between dimensions have become thinner, allowing us to more easily access who we truly are. Now is the time to tune into your soul, to listen, and pay attention to what your soul has to say. Thomas Moore wrote a book called *Care of the Soul*, and in it he states "The mind thinks, the body acts, and the soul imagines." The soul imagines love and joy and with conscious connection increases creativity. Listen for a message from your soul about your particular purpose on the planet during these times of change.

We are the catalyst of our intent that allows our Higher Self to select what we need. Since we are infinite beings, we are safe. There is no reason to fear. We are just morphing into a new way of being. We are on our way to integrating out of physical and into divine bodies. What a ride it will be, what an adventure, what a way to *live*.

Perhaps what you have read resonates with you on some level, or on many levels, or not at all. Are you looking for a sign? They are everywhere and tell us of the coming days. You just have to tune in to them and begin to understand their significance.

What in The World Is Going On?

We are actually in training to change our own perceptions, to allow certain new energies to exist in our reality. We are changing our paradigm. Now more than ever before it is the time to trust your intuition and energies from deep within yourself—to learn what your bliss is.

So much upheaval is taking place on so many levels—the world economy, leadership, global warming. These are key indicators that reveal that something significant is happening.

By now we are familiar with, most likely on a personal basis, what is happening with the economy. Great shifts are taking place almost daily on the worth of companies, bank accounts, trade, and money. These crises are present in the world because they are a response to humans using and abusing sacred powers. This too is a sign that something extraordinary is about to happen. The principle of integrity in economics is starting to help grow our financial system. Look for this to continue to be used in all business to prune away those that are not in integrity. And try not to believe everything the media tells you. It is, after all, just one perspective, one way of thinking. You get to choose whether or not you want to make it your "reality."

There was a tremendous shift in leadership when Barack Obama was elected president of the United States. Not only was change his message, but it signified a great change in leadership itself. Every one in the country felt it—of course, not in exactly the same way.

In addition, great changes are happening in the leadership in the Middle East. Even five years ago, who could have predicted that regimes in Tunisia, Egypt, and Bahrain could have fallen? Some of these changes took place rapidly, others continue to be drawn out. It is a part of the Lightworker's mission to hold the highest and best for the peoples of these countries. As of this writing the turmoil continues in Libya.

Global warming is happening from the inside out. Think of all the energies that bombard the earth through the opening in the magnetic field. Those energies pass through us, but also through the earth, down to the core. What effect are they having on the earth?

In early 2002, a very large chunk of ice collapsed and broke away from the Antarctic Peninsula. It was named Larsen B, and it was just slightly larger than the state of Rhode Island. It was very high and very deep. It was predicted that it would melt slowly, taking several years. It melted in less than three months—between January 31 and March 7—and sent out smaller icebergs.

Personal Transitions

Think about the changes that have occurred in your own neighborhood. How many have lost jobs and/or careers and had to reinvent themselves or are in the process of doing so?

Another change that is occurring is that many people are choosing to leave the planet and make their transition into the non-physical—especially but not exclusively older members of our world. There is a sense that they do not have the stamina for the time that is coming.

How many of you have had parents make this final transition? Think about your own family in the last two years and those around you. How many of the "older generation" in your family are still here? How many elderly neighbors have you noticed that are no longer living around or near you?

Crop Circles

Crop circles are not new. They have been around for hundreds of years. They have appeared in twenty-nine countries. While some may, or may not, have been proven to be hoaxes, the truth of the matter is, they can not all be fakes. Instead, consider that they might be a hieroglyphic or a pictograph, but instead of being carved in stone, they are carved in the fields of the earth. They are implanted with meaning.

Many believe that it is a series of energy waves that make the geometric shapes—some of them quite complex. For instance, one crop circle was created in Avebury Manor on July 15, 2008. Researchers came to the conclusion that it was an accurate rending of how the solar system will appear on December 21, 2012.

As we speed up toward the shift in consciousness, crop circles are a way for higher beings to communicate with us through the use of symbolism—most notably sacred geometry. The message for all of us? To live in the Light!

Many people believe that the crop circles are written in The Language of Light. This language is the original language of creation and resonates with us on a very deep level. It is constructed on concepts that are reflected in shape, color, and tone. Over time on Earth, the tones of creation became distorted, and then destruction and separatism became prevalent on Earth. The Language of Light is the original glyphs, tones, and vibrations utilized on Earth prior to the distortion.

If you have ever heard anyone speak in the Language of Light (and there are some today that can) it is an amazing experience. We hold these tones in our consciousness and when heard it can strike a very deep emotional chord within us. Other people have the same emotional response when they see the glyphs in crop circle. The Language of Light is based on unity consciousness where there are no destructive thought forms.

Freddy Silva in his book *Secrets In The Fields* asks the following questions:

What if you were given a set of keys that awaken a worldwide, sleeping network of energy, that access a library of ancient information, that encode new systems of technology, bring with them the power to heal, to alter consciousness and affect social change? What if these keys provided a bridge between the physical and non-physical realms? What if those keys could ultimately unlock the Universal potential within all of us?

Gregg Braden in his book *The God Code* states that "each cell and DNA strand is encoded. We are living libraries."

Cosmic Events

The largest and biggest event we will all experience takes place on the winter solstice in December of 2012. The earth will cross the equator of the Galactic Center of our universe. Our planet will pass by a black hole—not close enough to get sucked in, but close enough to have a very significant experience. This is an astronomical event on more than one level. It is a regular cycle that occurs every twenty-six thousand years. As there is no recorded history from the last time this happened, there is much discussion over the meaning of this event.

Most of it comes from an interpretation of the Mayan calendar. As most know by now, the Mayan long count calendar comes to an end on December 21, 2012. Some people believe this signifies the end of the world. Mayan expert Carl Johan Calleman explains it as follows:

It was the fulfillment of the prophecy of Quetzalcoatl, known as the Thirteen Heavens and Nine Hells. The prophecy stated that following the ninth hell, humanity would know and experience an unprecedented New

Age of Peace. The Hell cycle ended on August 16, 1987; the Harmonic Convergence began on August 17. Thus began the projected twenty-five year culmination of the 5,125 year Great Cycle of History, as well as the 26,000-year cycle of evolution, both slated to end in 2012. Time of The Harmonic Convergence was an announcement of the forthcoming end of time as we know it and a preparation to move from third-dimensional reality of space into fourth-dimensional reality of time.

In addition, there is an eleven-year cycle in which the sun sends out solar flares. The last time this took place was in May of 1999. The solar wind stopped for three days. This event will occur again in December 2012. NASA refers to the fact that the "sun is coming out of a slumber." In 2000 the magnetic field was perfect. Now it appears to be destabilizing which means, as of this writing, there is a large hole in the magnetic field of the earth.

This was a headline story on NASA's website:

On June 3, 2007 NASA's five THEMIS spacecraft discovered a breach in Earth's magnetic field ten times larger than anything previously thought to exist. Solar wind can flow in through the opening to "load up" the magnetosphere for powerful geomagnetic storms. But the breach itself is not the biggest surprise. Researchers are even more amazed at the strange and unexpected way it forms, overturning long-held ideas of space physics.

Dr. Michio Kaku, the well known theoretical physicist, and other scientists are concerned because it means that the x-rays and microwaves and other types of energy that bombards the earth is usually filtered through our magnetic field. It is not completely understood what is happening to the magnetic field of the earth. However, for some reason, the magnetic field is going away, allowing that energy to reach the earth, everyone and everything on it.

It is a common fact of life that we rely so much on technology just to function in our daily lives. For three days, the solar wind will stop, and the energy that comes through the black hole at the Galactic Center via the sun will permeate the Earth. Scientists are concerned about the satellites we have in space, the communication systems on earth, the Internet—every electronic device on the planet will be affected. They are warning as of this writing that companies and governments need to prepare now for this event. What they don't realize is that energy will also permeate each and every one of us as well.

The magnetic north moves. This has been going on since the mid-1800s. During the twentieth century, true north shifted at an average speed of 10 km per year, and within the last few years that has increased to about 40 km per year. At this rate it will exit North America and reach Siberia in a few decades.

This is not written to put you in a place of fear—that is a third-dimensional reality. But, rather, to get you to start thinking of what all these changes mean for us. What is the significance of those signs in our lives? These are tremendous energies that will be focused upon the earth. I believe I did mention that we are all made from energy. What impact will this have on all of us in relation to where we have been as a species and where we are going? Could there be a more perfect time to hear your soul's calling and realize we must move toward love and peace?

There are other cosmic events which will lead up to this event which will have a significant impact on the earth and those of us living upon it. For instance, we need to start paying attention to the energies associated with all equinoxes and all solstices, especially, but not only, 12-21-2012.

In 2010, there were two solar and two lunar eclipses. A partial lunar eclipse took place around the summer solstice, and a full lunar eclipse took place on the winter solstice. Both of these events usher in powerful energies onto the earth and offer catalytic trigger events that allow us to feel the result of these energies. Many more begin to wake up to the consciousness of what is happening to them and around them. The third-dimensional illusion is breaking down.

Think of the years of 2010-2012 as the "Grand Cross years." The June 26, 2010, eclipse conjoined Pluto and activated a grand cross involving the Sun,

Mercury, Jupiter, Uranus, the Moon, and Saturn. Astrologists say this was an important event with a huge impact on the energies of the earth. There have also been key eclipses that have brought in new energy.

On August 6 - 7, 2010, a cardinal grand cross formed which involved Jupiter-Uranus in Aries, Pluto in Capricorn, the Moon in early Cancer, and Venus joining Mars and Saturn in early Libra. Again, significant cosmic energies bombarded our planet. What we are facing is the activation of cosmic energies that penetrate our planet and signify a turning point in the evolution of our development as a species.

Satellites recording information from the Galactic Center show a wave of light in the path of earth that goes through its center in 2012. Right now this light is between the constellations Hydra and Centaurus. This energy will raise consciousness at a tremendous speed and line us up for our transition into the fifth dimension.

All of these events act as gateways to allow energy in to move us forward toward our receptivity to the fifth dimension.

Mother Earth Herself

Our planet is birthing this new dimension as well. The signs that she is in the very same evolutionary state are apparent with what is going on in the world. In 2010 alone there were numerous earthquakes all over the world of 6.0 or higher on the Richter scale. In January of 2010 there was an earthquake in Haiti that was 7.0 and took place at a depth of 8.1 miles. Even the aftershocks—of which there were many—ranged from 4.2 to 5.9 in strength. Since that time there have been earthquakes in Indonesia, the South Pacific, Japan, and South America.

In April of 2010 there was an oil disaster in the Gulf of Mexico of such magnitude it was unclear if they were ever going to be able to stop it. This was a wake-up call. Although we have come a long way in terms of our "green" consciousness, the message is clear that we still have a long way to go. We are out of balance with nature.

On another level, Mother Earth is giving birth to new consciousness as well. We will move into the fifth dimension, but so will she. The spilling of the oil in the Gulf could be considered the "breaking of the water," so to speak, of the beginning of the birthing process. The next few years will hold many changes for the earth, how we respond, how we value, hold, treasure, and treat our beloved planet will have much to say about whether this will be an easy birthing process or a hard one.

Recently, the most dramatic event of all occurred when there was an earthquake in Japan of the almost unimaginable magnitude of 9.0. This resulted in a tsunami that caused massive destruction and focused attention all over the world on the safety of nuclear power.

Thoughts are energy and combined with feeling can equal love or negativity. On still another level, we take our thoughts for granted when we think them. We just think what we think. However, if thoughts are things—and they are—where do they go after they are thought? The lower fourth dimension is the place where all collective thought goes that emanates from every living thing. Think about that for a moment. There are about six billion people on the planet. They all think every day, all day—many of them in fear. Their thoughts reside in the lower fourth dimension. This realm of thought bridges the physical, three-dimensional world that we take for granted and the unseen world of higher dimensions. These thoughts reside in the earth itself.

Why do you suppose right now that we have had so many events—earthquakes, floods, oil spills? Mother Earth is releasing and spewing out the gunk of all the negative thoughts and energies. Dense energy, negativity, negative thoughts sink, and lighter thoughts—love, things that make us feel good, laughter—rise and are more "airy." In preparation for what is going to happen in the next few years, the earth is clearing and releasing those thought forms and energies.

These are all symbols that are being sent to awaken our consciousness. Pains of birth of our Christ self adapting to a new way of experiencing the world can have moments of disorientation. Movies share this same message—*Avatar, The Last Airbender, Inception*. All thoughts are in the group consciousness and are expressed in many different ways. Some of them come out in our art forms.

In June of 2010 I attended a conference in Hot Springs, Arkansas. After working and doing much clearing and energy healing I fell into bed exhausted. Later that night I was awakened by a voice calling to me which said, "You Christed ones, now is the time to bring peace and glory back to earth." I got up and wrote that message down.

My prayer: show me the way; how can I help bring peace and glory back to earth? It was very shortly after that prayer that this book started to take off in composition and production.

Synchronicities

I know, allow, and surrender to a much greater power than I. This power and energy divinely guides my life. Many times I will say out loud, "I do not understand why I must do this, but I know there is a higher reason." Oftentimes, confirmation of what I am to do next or where I am to go comes through synchronistic encounters. Look for the synchronicities in your life.

On 9-9-09, it was no accident that I was present with many other Lightworkers on top of Mt. Magazine in Arkansas. As the Atlantis crystals were activated to Mother Earth, all the Lightworkers were welcomed—Arcturians, Pleiadians, and Sirians—seen and unseen. As I looked around the group I noticed that it was completely comprised of individuals all in my age range, and I cried in joy at this important event.

When I am ready to receive something, it appears or someone calls with the answer to where to go to find exactly what I need. I have come to expect this kind of synchronicity in my life and now I only smile when it happens.

How many synchronicities are happening right now in your life? How often do you run into people at the store whom you haven't seen for a while and then several days later you run into them again?

Think of all the events in your life as having some kind of meaning for you. Start paying attention to what happens in your own personal world. Think how often you want to speak to a particular person and then they call or email you. Begin to have faith in the divine process because our life becomes magic when we allow and surrender to our higher self.

When I do my work I often engage with people who share my birthday or the birthday of someone close to me. I often meet people with the same first name of important people in my life. Sometimes we are connected by a common friend or place, yet the two of us have never met. I immediately know that it was no accident that we came together. That it is a sign that we are both on the right course.

Finally, watch and observe the key dates in the next years that will be most important. They are 10-10-10, 11-11-11, and 12-12-12. Watch for events at Mt. Shasta and other special places on the planet as ceremonies are held and new and old healing energies are released.

Remember, if you continue to argue for your limitations the transition to the fifth dimension will be very hard for you. If you do desire the easy way, then release those things that no longer serve you—one of which is your sense of lack on any level. When you align with higher guidance, commit to love, harmony, and light; then you will attract that from those around you.

Exercise:

Keep an intuitive journal.

Pay attention to what gets your attention.

When you imagine something, and it works out that way, write it down, record it. Put as much detail into it as possible, particularly how you felt about it. Record what it was, how it unfolded, and what you felt the outcome was.

Watch carefully to see what happens as your intuitive abilities increase and synchronicities occur more often.

Affirmations:

I trust there is a greater conscious power that guides me when I listen.

I surrender to my Higher Self this day.

I allow divine flow to control and shift my energies for the highest and best.

I know that the divine plan for my life is moving forward.

As I step onto my divine golden pathway and purpose, I cannot see the outcome. I only trust that all is for the highest and best of all concerned in each situation.

I welcome divine magic into my life and recognize that all things are easily and effortlessly possible.

CHAPTER FIVE

We may explore the universe and find ourselves,
or we may explore ourselves and find the universe.
It matters not which of these paths we choose.

Diana Robinson

The Fifth Dimension Is Not Just A Vocal Group

———————————————

"Google" the 5th Dimension and you will come up with a preponderance of hits about the famous multiple Grammy-winning singing group. Certainly you have heard many of their hits, one of which is familiar to most people—the rendition of "Aquarius/Let the Sunshine In." A medley of two songs from the musical *Hair*, it was written based on the belief that the world would soon be entering the Age of Aquarius, an age of Love and Light.

Released as a single over forty years ago, it is the Divine Creator's great sense of humor that a group called the 5th Dimension would sing about the coming evolution of the Earth and everyone in it into the new reality of the fifth dimension—a dimension of Love and Light.

Awakening and Consciousness

What does it mean to be "Awake" or "Conscious"? In the medical sense there is no answer to this question. Consciousness from the viewpoint of modern medicine is not quite understood. Modern medicine only really understands the absence of consciousness or when you are unconscious. They call it death when consciousness is completely absent.

In a spiritual sense, it means to know who and what you truly are. Dr. Richard Bartlett, author of *Matrix Energetics*, defines us as light and consciousness. It means that you are more than what you have been taught or learned. Perhaps by this point you realize that or you already know it. You have taken the first step.

At first you may not recognize that you have made a shift. You will be resonating to a lighter, higher field of consciousness. Our spiritual development and our ability to hold a higher light will determine which vibratory dimension in which we will resonate.

Dimensions are not "out there." They are inside of us. We must first believe that we can experience the fifth dimension in our daily lives. Then the fifth dimension will fuel our light, not our density. We will no longer react to drama in our lives the same way. We will live in choice. Life will feel less complicated and more about service, grace, creativity, and enlightenment. We will easily have contact with our Higher Selves.

Right now on planet Earth there is a great Awakening going on. For many years we have accepted a third dimensional reality that has told us what you perceive through your five senses is reality. Now we are beginning to wake up to the fact that there is more. There is a knowing that does not come through our so-called "reality." We create our reality through our thought, feelings, and actions.

In a comparatively short amount of time—since the mid-nineteenth century—there have been hints that this form of knowledge existed. We see this in the transcendental movement of Thoreau and Emerson, the great age of Spiritualism in this country that lasted from the Civil War until World War I. We see it in the introduction of eastern thought into western culture. We see it in the introduction and use of Yoga, Reiki, psychic readings, energy healers, movies such as *The Sixth Sense*, television shows such as *The Ghost Whisperer* and *Touched By An Angel*, and, of course, the international phenomenon of _The Secret_. It has become mainstream to think about your spiritual life.

Is there a yearning within you? Is there recognition or restlessness that there has to be something more? Are you thirsty for knowledge? Perhaps you can't even articulate what that is. Perhaps you are awakening to your own spiritual path. Whatever that is, you are in for an exhilarating and exciting ride because all the changes in the world are accelerating.

Some Signals That You Are Awakening

Are you wondering about your purpose in life? Are you asking why you are here? Because your DNA has been disconnected for so long, you have forgotten so much. Are you starting to remember? Do the concepts in this book resonate with you? What do you *know*?

Is time speeding up for you? Are you finding less time in your day to accomplish your regular errands and work? Do you hardly wake up and then suddenly it's time for lunch? It seems you barely have time to turn around before you find yourself preparing dinner or looking for a restaurant. Then suddenly you are conscious that it is time for bed and you wonder where the day went.

Has your vision changed? Did you just get new glasses or contacts and feel that you need to have your vision checked again?

Has the pattern of your sleep cycle changed? Do you wake up in the middle of the night and look at your digital clock and see that it is somewhere between two and four in the morning? There are a lot of new energies bombarding the planet, and a lot of internal work is going on within you. Do you go back to sleep or get up? Do you need more or less sleep than usual? Are you napping during the day? Perhaps this is something you never did before.

Are you having very intense dreams? Are they in color with a lot of movement? Your dreams are helping you to let go of what no longer serves your highest good. They also help to release old energy patterns in preparation for the new energy that is almost upon us.

Do you feel physically disoriented at times? Do you find yourself driving your car and all of a sudden you realize you have forgotten where you are, where you are going, or how you got to where you are? Do you feel light or "spacey" at times? Do you have a sensation that you exist between two worlds and can't explain the feeling? If you can go into nature, sit and ground yourself and that will help you a great deal with those kind of feelings.

Are you experiencing more déjà vu experiences? Quantum physics now tells us something that most metaphysicians have always known. There are multi-universes based on that fact that all possibilities exist. The veils between the multi-universes are thinning, and sometimes you can get a look into those worlds and they look familiar to you. It may no longer seem random that you meet people who feel familiar and realize certain synchronicities in your lives.

How is your memory? Do you remember things easily that happened some time ago in your past? If not, don't worry, you don't have Alzheimer's disease. You are releasing those things that are no longer important to you. You are starting to live in the now.

What's happening in your life? Going through a divorce? Having serious money issues? Relationship issues? Work issues? Are things splitting apart and coming together in ways that you could never have imagined would ever take place in your life? You are mirroring what is happening on Mother Earth. As she goes through all the changes—the tsunamis, earthquakes, hurricanes, fires, and floods—so do you also experience the equivalent of upheaval in your life. As difficult as it may be to go through whatever you are experiencing, know that you are shifting your energies to a higher vibrational frequency and letting go of what no longer serves you.

Do you sometimes feel that you just want to go home? This is not an impulse to end it all. It is a feeling that you are done. You've completed all your tasks and would like it to be over. If you are hearing this call you need to consider that you may be part of the mission to help others make the journey into the new energy. Just like you found this book, others can learn about the coming age from you. I promise it will be well worth it in the end. Many subtle energies are coming in now of which we are completely unaware.

I want to assure you that the most exciting part is ahead of us. Don't walk out of the theater before the end of the movie!

Are you more aware of your environment? Does what surrounds you feel good or feel bad? Are you navigating your daily life into energies that feel good? Refrain from moving in any direction that feels bad to you. Set your intent to find things during your day that makes you feel good.

There are other symptoms as well, and you really need to tune into the changes you perceive in our own life instead of ignoring them. So much new energy is coming onto the planet at this time that you may be responding in ways that you are shrugging off as age, the environment, or issues in your daily life. Stop for a moment and think. How has your body, your mind, your psyche changed? Are you responding to impulses you really don't understand? These are all signals that dramatic change is coming, and you are awakening to spiritual consciousness and the true significance of that change.

Welcome to the journey into the next evolution of the Earth. You are feeling that birthing process right in your own body.

The Exciting Time in Which We Live

So much change is happening for the better. Every single one of us is here for some reason to participate in the emergence of the planet into the Light.

If you are familiar with the size and shape of the fifty trillion cells in your body—all wonderfully performing the many different functions that make YOU the physical being you are—then you know they have a roundish shape. As they begin to become crystalline in nature, they will reform into the shape of two pyramids base to base—or the octahedron. This is the sacred geometry of our cells.

This is why clearing is so important. We have to release our karmic past on every level. The very core of our cellular structure is changing—bringing in more minerals. This is happening so that our cells transform from the simple carbon structure we know into an organic crystalline structure that will allow them to hold more light.

That is why mastering the third and fourth dimensions is so important—and it is important to master them with *awareness*. As you think and feel it will manifest *immediately* in the fifth dimension. This has significant consequences for the reality you create around you. You must be at the point where you can control your thoughts and emotions and focus them in positive and uplifting ways.

This does not mean that you no longer have thoughts and emotions. It means that you must train yourself to release negative reactions to events and conditions. Begin to observe situations around you as a witness without allowing your emotions to rule you. Do not go into drama. When someone cuts you off the highway, you can choose to follow them at "ramming speed" or you can choose to let it/them go. Instead, God bless them, pray for their safety and those they encounter.

When you suffer some setback or another you can rail against your unlucky stars or bemoan that things always "happen" to you or you can step back and honor the feelings but not go "to" the feeling. Allow that the particular experience you are having is interesting and then ask yourself, "How can I feel better about this? Where did this come from in my feeling nature?" Find the next best feeling you can reach for and live in that.

That energy of the shift in 2012 will completely alter the particles on Earth. For human beings, the electrons that make up the smallest part of us— the atoms of our bodies—will have more space between them. The planet will be re-patterned. Our bodies will be re-patterned.

This is the ascension process. Metaphysically, we ascend to a time of Love, a *consciousness* of Love. We will be the *embodiment* of Love.

Everyone has the opportunity to ascend. Everyone has the opportunity to clear away the old energy of the past, the negativity, the hatred, the blame, the fears and move into the next step of evolution on planet Earth. Everyone has the opportunity to create their Heaven. Each person's Heaven may be different, on different levels or perceptions of the fifth dimension, but all will be based on the energies of love and light.

However, freewill exists. Those who have no interest or intention in moving towards the light will not be able to exist in the energies which will be the new norm. They may physically die and reincarnate in another place where the energies will be similar so that their soul can continue to learn and grow as is appropriate for them. There is no judgment; each of us is on our separate journey back to the Divine Creator, learning at our own rate. No one is lost. Each person will have her or his own result based upon how clear that person is, how much in the light she or he is, and how able she or he is able to receive the new energies. My work clears the four bodies to allow the highest light to shine from the soul and connect.

The advent of this shift has already arrived, creating a foreshadowing of a way of being on the planet that is based in love, not just survival—one that seeks to serve the good of all rather than the desires of self. Such a movement has God at the center by whatever name God is called, for the movement itself does not belong to any nation, religious tradition, or group.

What Does the Fifth Dimension Mean?

The fifth dimension is a realm of light on every level of beingness and consciousness. It centers on the human heart, and it is in harmony with *all* of life on the planet.

Until we go within ourselves, nothing that we seek, nothing that we do externally will be in the fifth dimension. This can be painful because when trying to achieve mastery of the fifth dimension we must realize exactly what is there. Unconditional love. Living on purpose. You are mastering love at its highest point, mission work and service for God at the highest point. If you back down, you will keep getting painful lessons, over and over again until you understand their significance and move on. Sometimes knowing it and thinking it, you have to get confirmation within yourself in order to move forward.

Know that in the fifth dimension, you are enough. You are whole. You are worthy. Nothing is broken. Nothing needs to be fixed. Knowing something and learning it are two different steps in the process. When it drops down to your heart and you *feel* the truth of it, you have moved forward because coming in touch with our intuitive nature reaffirms our "knowing." It is through our heart that we begin to think—by *feeling* our true nature of unconditional love.

What is unseen in the third dimension will now be seen in the fifth dimension.

There's a good possibility that you now find fear when seeking your mission but as you evolve into your heart and the fifth dimension, you *know* you can do it. You *want* to do it. You *must* to do it. So you keep stepping out one step at a time. Everyone is on a different growth curve. If you consider our lives 100 percent growth and 100 percent service on the highest level—without martyrdom or victimhood—then, there is only love in what and who you are.

Living from the Right Brain

Historically speaking, we are a Left Brain world. We have concentrated on all those aspects of logic, system, control, "reality." In the fifth dimension, that will no longer serve us. We will shift to a Right Brain world in which intuition, feeling, creativity, love will be honored. We will live from Creativity, Inspiration, and Knowing. What great joy we will find with ourselves and others.

Lower frequencies such as fear and limitation cannot exist in the fifth dimension. We will live in our "Christ Consciousness," a consciousness of unconditional love. We will surrender to the spirit that resides inside every cell of our beings.

The Importance of the Heart Chakra

The power in the fifth dimension comes from your feelings. For in the fifth dimension, you live out of this most important Chakra, your heart Chakra. You cannot be in the fifth-dimension consciousness unless your heart Chakra is wide open. The fifth dimension is all about love and living from the heart and the soul and listening to the heart and soul. Being willing to listen to the heart instead of the mind is our first step into the fifth dimension. Your heart is intelligent and compassionate. You must learn to trust it. The heart is knowledge; the heart can even see if you allow it. Let your heart help you to discover the new world as it unfolds. Let your heart be your guide.

You must begin to think with the heart. What does that mean? The rational mind has been a protection, a device for living in the third dimension so you can survive. That will no longer exist. The heart connects you to divine love which is unconditional. The heart connects you to your Higher Self. Every heart (the feeling/knowing in you) contains God's spark. It is up to you to nourish that spark with love instead of blocking the heart and soul when in fear. The heart energy is blocked when you experience the energies of fear and doubt or are obsessive about the judgment of others.

We all know that your brain has an electromagnetic field. Did you know that your heart also has one? It is five thousand times greater than the one your brain possesses. While your thoughts are important, what is the value of your feelings? Heart and higher mind connect in a clearing and DNA reconnection. Your power opens to use that incredible magnetic field to attract and heal yourself and others.

Think now of the moments in your life when you could not speak, only *feel*. We have all had those moments. Recall them for yourself now.

Remember the feeling now you might have had when

- You first looked into the eyes of your new-born child.
- You stood at your wedding ceremony and made a commitment.
- You sat at the deathbed of a loved one.
- You were taken totally by surprise by another's kindness and demonstration of love for you.
- You fell in love for the first time.
- You had your heart broken.

Living from the heart teaches us forgiveness, compassion, creativity, trust, imagination, wisdom. Only when the heart is open and surrendered to the Divine does the heart access wisdom beyond time and "a peace that surpasses understanding." It is living in the fifth dimension of consciousness.

What events have triggered the opening of your heart? 9/11? The BP oil crisis? The tsunami in Indonesia or perhaps the earthquakes in Haiti or Japan? Something in your own community that has happened may have been your call to service—your school, your church, your community, your state, or the region in which you live. Was it caring for an animal or neighbor who was ill? Was it volunteering at some event or recognition of what is taking place in the world as a whole?

What moves you emotionally is easy for you to commit to because of that movement in your heart. Not your head, your heart. It is from our hearts that we ultimately make our life decisions because this is the symbolic center of the now.

Relationships

Relationships are a key example of this. If your heart Chakra is not ready for a relationship, then you are not going to have anybody in your life. If you do not love yourself, if you are expecting to find somebody else to open up your heart, it is not going to happen. If your heart is not open to yourself, it is not going to be open to anybody else. Nobody else is going to want to be there with you. Over and over I teach this energy every week to clients who so long for a partner in their lives.

"A loving relationship isn't about finding the right person; it's about being the right person." Gregg Braden – The Isaiah Effect.

What you do with your heart Chakras is a vibrational frequency that draws to you the light frequency of others at the same vibrational level. You cannot just say, "I'm going to find my partner!" First you have to be *ready* for a partner. Your heart Chakra has to be ready.

I spoke with a man who had been divorced for eight years. He had been so hurt—really damaged by his relationship with his former wife. He was raising two little boys by himself and his heart Chakra was only 60 percent open! He had closed down because of the painful relationship that he had experienced. I told him there was a woman there for him, that she was ready for him, but that he had to open his heart Chakra and love in order for her to come to him because *he was not ready for her.*

Money

When I receive money for anything I do, I like to hold the hand of the person who is giving me money with the money between our hands. I pray, thanking all the people and the higher beings that brought in this higher energy for healing, for allowing me to be a channel. I pray for the person and his/her higher beings and guides for bringing this monetary energy and gifting it to me. It is a two-way street—give and take. My clients recognize this and energetically they get it more than anything else. Money is energy too—a form of appreciation—and I have something to offer as they offer to me. We are *gifting* the energy back and forth as we appreciate one another.

Once the truth of this gifting and appreciation for one another is recognized it can make a dynamic shift in consciousness about money. This does not only work with money. You can do this with *anything* that you give and receive. However, work on your faith and money will come. First appreciate what you already have. It will open the doors for more for you to appreciate. You must *feel* rich to be rich. Part of everything I do is shifting conscious belief systems. Sometimes it is big and sometimes it is just over small things.

Health

The physical manifestation of any illness starts in the spiritual realm. It could be described as a disturbance in your own personal force—stress, feelings of being less than, living in fear, "should-ing" on yourself. Eventually all of these negative energies manifest in some form or another in the physical.

These are the lies which we have told ourselves: 1) I am unworthy to be loved by the Divine Creator which causes sadness, 2) I am all alone here which causes fear, and 3) I have been betrayed, abandoned by the Divine Creator which causes anger.

You have the power to heal yourself once you begin to love yourself. Love is the most powerful energy in the entire universe. Your soul is composed of it. Its essence is the Divine Creator. It is the only thing that is real. All else is illusion. Learn from the inside what emotion comes up in any situation. It is a lie. Talk to yourself to remove the illusion, to wake up to truth. Love your ego into wholeness. Be your ego's parent and wise one. The ego is often very childish many times and needs attention. Therefore, true healing is always done with and through love.

Part of the enlightenment is just the awareness of the vibrational frequencies that are all around us. You can actually practice with that—just feeling—animals, flowers, plants, any living thing. Everything—even a rock has a vibrational frequency (albeit a very dense one). If you hold a crystal and wait a moment, you will feel the pulse of it.

Some of the crystals are downloaded with certain frequencies and certain information that you can gather from them if you can tune your energies into the energies of the rock and listen and ask that it be downloaded. I've taken crystals and before I give them to people I download love energy. I ask that love be downloaded into the crystal and then, without telling the person I give the crystal to, I just tell them it's very special and that they need to put it by their bed or on their desk. Particularly for people who are not conscious, it is a way for them to feel higher energy or feel love.

Just Do It

All excuses are invalid. All work is about the energy. So if you feel you are too young, too old, too big, too small, too rich, too poor. If you have the "too's" you must begin to release that and realize it is all about where you vibrate your energy on a certain topic. Perfect health is available to you. Absolute prosperity is available to you. The right and perfect partner to share your life is available to you. It is all available now through the love that you are and the love you transmit.

Do the things that encourage you to open your heart to others now. Practice surrendering to something larger than yourself. Recognize that everything, and I mean every thing, is in Divine Order. If you can integrate what you have learned and experienced with love then you truly create a celestial experience in your own life.

Get into the "zone" for whatever you do. When you are in your bliss you create the world you want. If you don't feel that for your job, get into the place where you do feel it—with your partner, your child, your volunteer work, how you feel when you work in your garden. Be in that place, that feeling experience of love, and then apply it when you are in those places and situations when you can not so clearly feel it. "Fake it until you make it."

Begin now to seek understanding with whom you interact with. Give up watching and listening to the media. It is just someone's perspective on what is happening in three-dimensional reality. The more you pay attention to that, the more you mire yourself in that level of consciousness. Listen to those who seek you out. They have a message for you, and you have information for them. Be present for the ones you love and those who you encounter. Do not abdicate your responsibility. Once you have awakened and are conscious to what is happening, you cannot go back. You must go forward. Start to let go of the things around you that have no real meaning for you. Any possessions you have that were just acquired for the purpose of having more no longer serve you. Just take what you need. Surrender to your Higher Self. Know that all is in Divine Order.

Thought travels faster than light; love travels even faster than thought. Be love. Be the love you already are. The fifth dimension is the place of true celestial being. It is the place in which we create Heaven on Earth. Therefore, look for ways to reduce the stress of those around you. Ask yourself, "In what ways can I express my soul today?"

What loving acts of random kindness can you perform? These don't have to be very big at all—just opening the door for someone can have significance. Just smiling at a stranger or letting someone else go first in line has impact. Every life experience we undergo is an opportunity to practice unconditional love. Practice patience with people you meet in stores or with the customer service people with whom you interact. I always tell people that I appreciate their patience with me. I always make sure I thank people for whatever they have done for me and compliment them on how well they have done it.

Remember, this concept resonates from who you are at your core. Your purpose will soon be to express unconditional love and there is no reason you cannot begin that right now. Remember, the Law of Attraction is always at work. If you broadcast that you love and honor yourself, others will resonate with that and follow suit. *You train people how to treat you by the way you treat yourself.*

If you love and honor yourself, if you verbalize that, others will respond to that and follow your lead.

Exercise:

Ask your Higher Self for the vision of your life. You can do this by requesting assistance in identifying your path based on the highest outcome and the most love. It is not enough that you merely ask for "help." You must be particular and specific.

Invoke the clear white light of the Divine Creator. Surround yourself with this light and from this place ask your Higher Self, "Please assist me in figuring out how to complete _____ for my work."

Ask yourself, "Am I willing and ready to go beyond fear in the world and let love be my guide?" Pay attention; choose the world that you wish to live in. You will see that your consciousness will begin to direct what you choose for yourself in life. When God is love there is only the present moment and its power. Only in the present moment is our power.

As your intuition wakes up and becomes active, you will begin to have a sense when things you want to happen are about to unfold. You may wish to record your feelings and sensations as well as when and how they work out. As you keep track of your intuitive "hits" they will begin to happen more often. This particularly works well after asking for help. That help will come in the form of guidance which may be small or large. Take note of it, follow it, and see what comes from it.

Affirmations:

I am perfect love.

I love myself for stepping into my Divine mission.

I intend to live each moment listening and allowing perfection of love and light to transform my life.

CHAPTER SIX

Sacred Geometry is the form beneath our being and points to
a divine order in our reality. We can follow that order from
the invisible atom to the infinite stars, finding ourselves at each step.

Drunvalo Melchizedek

What's Sacred About Geometry?

Most of us have distinct memories about taking geometry in high school. Today it is a subject for middle school children. In any case, no one ever felt there was anything sacred about the Pythagorean Theorem. But geometry is taught because it is so important on so many levels. Have you ever wondered why? It is not until you start really looking around you that you begin to understand the elegance of geometry.

Think of sacred geometry as another kind of language that everyone understands and can respond to. At its very heart, it describes the perfection of nature and the order of the universe. It encompasses the recognizable shapes that unite all forms of life. Think of anything from a starfish to a sunflower, the cells in our bodies, all the way to the motions of the planets and the stars—everything has a geometric template and everything is linked one part to another. It is not about "doing the math." It is about looking around you and appreciating the perfection of it all.

Order, Not Chaos

Sacred geometry is an ancient art and science that reveals the nature of our relationship to everything else. As you become aware of the forms around you and begin to study them, it becomes apparent that there is a principle of unity that underlies all of creation—no matter how it is expressed. Everything is connected. This attention and appreciation unfolds the principle of oneness underlying all creation in its myriad expression and leads us inevitably to the perspective of interconnectedness, inseparability, and union.

These days it is hard to appreciate the order in our lives. So much seems in chaos. But when we look to nature, we always find patterns and designs that we can see. These patterns always follow geometrical structures which reveal the form of everything we perceive. These range in everything from the strands of our DNA to the designs of the sacred sites of the world—from Stonehenge and the Great Pyramid at Giza to some of the worlds' greatest places of worship.

Sacred geometry is essential to the learning process of the spiritual nature of our being.

The Platonic Solids

Over 2500 years ago Plato devised a theory about the earth's basic structure. He believed it evolved from a simple geometric shape to more complex shapes. They became known as the platonic solids. It was taught that these five perfect three-dimensional forms were the foundation of everything in the physical world and were therefore sacred.

All of them are polyhedrons, solid forms bounded by three or more line segments:

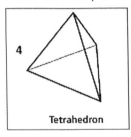

Tetrahedron

The tetrahedron with four faces.

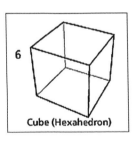

Cube (Hexahedron)

The hexahedron or Cube with six faces.

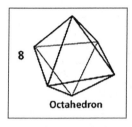

The octahedron with eight faces.

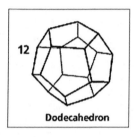

The dodecahedron has twelve.

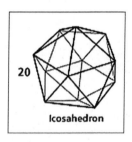

And the icosahedron has twenty faces.

When you experience these forms, it usually triggers something within you. Think about these forms and become cognizant of how apparent they are in your own life. They are expressed in everything in nature—from the flowers and leaves on the trees in your backyard to the very cells of your body. There is an *order* to the Universe—and each and every one of us, in our own unique way, is a part of that order.

Pyramid Sites

There are pyramid sites all over the world. While we are most familiar with the forms in Egypt and Mexico, pyramids have been found everywhere from China to Russia, Europe, and South America. The ancients used these patterns because they represented the sacred inner world of spirituality. Tremendous energy is expressed through these buildings because they are aligned to constellations and to some stars in particular thus forming a pathway for those energies to manifest.

One such example is the Temple of the Plumed Serpent in Chichén Itza. It is precisely aligned to the sun. As light hits the pyramid on the Spring and Autumn Equinox each year, the shadows from the corner tiers begin to form a series of seven isosceles triangles. As the day continues, the light creates the shadow of a serpent that seems to slither 120 feet down along the northern side of the pyramid with the sun's movement until it illuminates the large stone head of a snake at the base. People come from all over the world just to be there to witness this event.

In addition, many modern designers have used this shape for contemporary buildings. Consider the Luxor Hotel in Las Vegas, the Ryugyong Hotel in North Korea, or the Transamerica Building in San Francisco—as much a landmark as the Golden

Gate Bridge. All are based on the pyramid structure.

Just look a picture of a pyramid and then observe how it makes you *feel*.

Healing Modalities

Viewing and contemplating these forms can allow us to gaze directly at the face of deep wisdom and glimpse the inner workings of The Universal Mind. The forms of Sacred Geometry are often found in temples and cathedrals. These forms evoke something deep within us that unites us to the infinity of the cosmos and the beauty and balance of our world. Churches, Temples, and Cathedrals are not only places of worship but also offer a home for meditation and reflection. Sacred Geometry is often found in these places because it is the vehicle in which we can communicate with the universe through that reflection.

The Flower of Life

The Flower of Life expression encompasses many of the forms of sacred geometry. It is found in variations all over the world.

The Flower of Life is a geometrical figure composed of multiple evenly-spaced and over-lapping circles. They form a flower-like pattern with a six-fold symmetry like a hexagon. In other words, the center of each circle is on the circumference of six surrounding circles of the same diameter. The oldest example of the Flower of Life can be found at the Temple of Osiris at Abydos, Egypt.

Other examples can be found in Phoenician, Assyrian, Indian, Asian, Middle Eastern, and medieval art. A Flower of Life pattern can be constructed with a pen, compass, and paper, by creating multiple series of interlinking circles.

The Flower of Life is said to express the energy grid that covers the earth. We can key into these energy lines and by so doing, heal the planet. The Flower of Life has thirteen circles. If the center of each circle center is considered a "node," and each node is connected to each other node with a single line, a total of seventy-eight lines are created. Within this cube, many other shapes can be found, including two-dimensionally flattened versions of the five platonic solids.

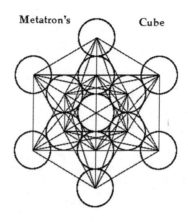

The Flower of Life pattern contains the basis of Metatron's Cube. From this pattern, all five of the Platonic solids can be derived.

Spirals

Pi

Pi, as we were all taught in grade school, is a number approximately equal to 3.14159. It is the ratio of the circumference of a circle to its diameter and is represented by the symbol π.

The phi spiral is a common geometry and proportion found in nature. The conch nautilus is an excellent example of the phi.

Spirals are easily found in nature. Just look at a sunflower, a pinecone, or the shell of a snail. Or look at your own fingerprints—all spirals.

Spirals are found in many sacred energy places, symbolizing portals into altered states and dimensions. They are etched in stone and found all over the world at sacred sites including Newgrange in Ireland.

What spins on our earth and in life? The earth itself spins on an axis. Hurricanes, tornadoes spin. A pendulum spins, and children love to spin. The planets spin, the galaxy spins, as well as the cosmos itself.

The Vortexes in different parts of the world— including those found outside of Sedona—are spirals. They represent expansion and evolution. They are gateways in the manifestation of spirit into matter. This form is seen in a lot of contemporary jewelry for this reason.

Ancient Signs and Symbols

Crop circles were mentioned in the chapter on Signs, but they also have a place in Sacred

Geometry. Geometric shapes speak to us in a special language—when they form certain shapes they evoke something within us. So you could consider crop circles a form of highly intelligent communication.

It has been shown that some crop circles encode obscure theorems based on Euclidian geometry. They are also invisibly encoded with sacred geometry—those harmonic ratios that govern the relationship between the orbits of planets in our solar system.

Sacred Geometry is a tool to for you to use to connect to the Divine Creator and to recognize the divine within yourself.

Exercise:

Start spinning!

Spread your arms and move from left to right. Like a dancer, focus your eye on an object so that you can return to it each time you finish a rotation. Start gradually—only performing three or four rotations—so that you can overcome any dizziness you may feel at the beginning. Gradually add more until you can spin twenty-one times per day.

Exercise:

Start paying attention to the forms around you.

Look for sacred geometry in your daily life and events.

If you dream of geometric forms it is an indication that sacred geometry is working within you. Keep track of these dreams and any specific shapes and colors that appear in them.

Go out in nature—really look at a flower or a tree or some aspect of your yard—the leaf of your favorite tree, for example—and see how the platonic solids are at work in your life.

If you attend church, pay attention to how geometry has been used in the architecture. Look for evidence of the platonic solid forms mentioned above.

Affirmation:

Life flows through the Universe, through me, and through my heart.

CHAPTER SEVEN

I honor the place in you in which the entire Universe dwells.
I honor the place in you which is of love, of truth, of light and of peace.
When you are in that place in you, I am in that place in me. We are one.

A translation of the Sanskrit "Namaste"

Are We Clear?

Preparing for the Shift into the fifth dimension is all about clearing and cleansing all the negative energies in your four energy bodies and reconnecting the strands of your DNA. The purpose of this process is to allow more light into your body. I will cover the topic of DNA in another chapter, but want to explain the importance of clearing now.

As a Lightworker, it is my mission to hold the highest light for others to see. I have always been aware of and susceptible to other people's pain. It took me a long time to understand that I am a "sensitive" and what that meant. It then became necessary for me to learn how to shift my intention about my ability to key into other's pain in order to use if for my highest and best good and to allow me to do the same for others. It became apparent to me that I had to shine the light within me so that others could begin to see their own light.

I have the ability to sense people's souls and know how clear they are, how much light their souls contain. I can check anybody, anywhere, any place in the world at any time. It is possible for me to connect to any being. It is my purpose to up-lift others and in order to do so I must hold a great deal of energy in my body so that the process of clearing can take place. My highest blessing is to be able to work with people, to help them clear out the dark energies and let them allow more light into their souls. A beautiful matrix exists around my energy fields that allows me to connect to the sixth dimension and to higher beings who work through me to heal and clear energy.

You Are More Than Your Physical Body

By now you understand that everything in the universe is made of energy. We are actually four energy bodies overlapping with a soul in the center of them. Think of your energy bodies as somewhat like four of those Russian dolls—all nesting one inside the other. Instead of wood, these bodies are invisible and are made of invisible energy (except, of course, for the very visible physical body). Because these four bodies vibrate at different frequencies, we are unable to see three of these bodies but each one, the physical, mental, emotional, and spiritual, store issues as patterns in your aura—the field of energy, in layers, that surrounds you.

The Physical Body

We are not just the body we see in the mirror every morning when we brush our teeth. Our physical body is not the only one we have; it is just the most apparent because it is so dense. It has height, breadth, and, for some of us, too much width. The physical body vibrates at a lower frequency than the other bodies, and our eyes translate that frequency into what we see in the mirror. We also use the rest of our senses to interpret this body. For many of us we take our physical body for granted until something goes wrong with it—until we experience distress or pain with it. We have all seen diagrams of what is inside our physical bodies, but for the most part we do not care to admit that we are flesh and bone and blood, but we know the truth of it.

When something has gone wrong in the other energy bodies of our aura, it manifests in the physical body.

The other three bodies we each possess are not often recognized.

The Mental Body

Thoughts become things, and they are very powerful. This is the energetic layer of the body in which attitudes, beliefs, thoughts, and ideas reside. What we are thinking about is cyclical— when you think, you analyze and those thoughts circle around and remain on this level.

Layers of emotional energies will respond to your thoughts from your mental body and imagination.

The Emotional Body

The Emotional Body encompasses all of your feelings. It is in this body that all your desires, moods, feelings, appetites, and fears reside. The emotional "self" goes hand in glove with the mental "self" allowing the emotional body to *express* the thoughts of the mental body. Think of your emotional body as a kind of pathway that links the mind and the physical body. Your fears, hopes, love, and pain all reside in the emotional body. It has a tremendous influence on the expression of your personality through the physical body.

The Spiritual Body

The Spiritual Body is associated with your true spiritual path and direction in life. It is here that your highest potential resides. This body reflects your ability to manifest the soul contract that you came to complete here on earth. We can recognize that this layer of energy contains and relates to intuition, knowingness, and guidance. This is a powerful layer because it coordinates the various responses of the other three bodies. Right now, if this resonates with you it is because it makes a great deal of sense to your Spiritual Body.

When I perform a clearing, I do not work with the four bodies separately. As I work, all the bodies are cleared at the same time. The four bodies vibrate at different frequencies. They are made up of etheric material. Because they each vibrate at different frequencies, it is possible to change those frequencies through your intentions. Our personal frequency is the sum total of all four bodies.

The Soul

The soul is connected to all four bodies. One of the things I am privileged to be able to do is *see* souls and *feel* the light in souls. There are some souls that feel wonderful to be near. As more people come into contact with their own energy fields, you will be able to feel the same thing—to feel the divinity, the higher consciousness, that is part of living in the fourth and fifth dimensions. The ability to sense the consciousness of what surrounds you is wonderful indeed. Sometimes I can feel souls that are familiar, even from past lives and that feels especially good.

A Woman in the Pain of a Bad Relationship

One day a woman called me. Her voice was so despondent, so strained. She felt that she was unable to think straight. She was having problems with her ex-husband and even though they were divorced, he continued to try to control her life through threats and negative actions. Needless to say, she felt overwhelmed because now he was in the process of attempting to take her house away from her. She did not know where to turn. While she wanted to have nothing more to do with him, she could not seem to get rid of him or the power he attempted to exert over her.

We spent several hours on the phone going through the process outlined below. After her session, she had a very difficult time de-tox-ing. She was sick in bed for a week with flu-like symptoms. Every one of her four energy bodies needed relief and were purging. She began to wonder who really loved her. She couldn't think straight (mental), she cried continuously (emo-tional), she had flu-like symptoms (physical), and she felt afraid.

She called me and asked me what I could do to decrease the discomfort of de-tox. I told her she was dehydrated and needed more water as well as thirty minutes a day of sun on her face. She took my advice and improved. The first thing that she became aware of was that she started to feel detached from the situation with her ex-husband so that she could feel and think more clearly.

After she gained back her personal power, she sent me a text that read," I feel like I've been touched by an angel, that's the good feeling I have."

An Overview of the Chakras

In Sanskrit, Chakra means "energy wheel." Chakras are very important to the process of clearing because these wheels, or vortexes, must be kept in motion, and that motion should be easy and effortless.

There are seven energy wheels in your body. They work up from the base of your spine, and the energy that floats around and through them moves in a serpentine pattern that interfaces with the four energy bodies. I can assess a lot about a person by the rate of spin of their Chakras. I ask for healing when needed, and on occasion I have to ask for a pillar of divine light to be inserted through the center of the Chakras to help support and allow for divine healing.

The higher Chakras deal with topics related to the spiritual realm, while the lower Chakras deal with the physical realm. When I work on opening the Chakras, I can sense and then check the percentage of energy that is in spinning through each one.

The Seventh Chakra – The Crown Chakra

The Seventh Chakra is the connection between the physical world and the world of spirit. Here resides the desire to experience life and the universe as one. You are able to communicate with your Higher Self and receive inspiration and revelations through this Chakra. This vortex, when clear and functioning, activates wisdom and understanding. It is located just above the crown of your head.

In most of the people I have encountered, the Crown Chakra is usually open. On the seldom occasion that the crown Chakra is not open, it may mean that there are knots in the silver cord that is your connection to God and God energy. Occasionally, it is necessary to replace the silver cord, but more likely it needs to be repaired. In cases like that I ask for healing of the cord and then I recheck the Chakra.

The Sixth Chakra - The Third Eye Chakra

The Sixth Chakra concerns psychic ability and intuition. It is no accident that the "sixth sense" is attributed to the sixth Chakra. This is the energy vortex that goes beyond the regular five senses and transcends time and space. It is the seat of extra sensory perception and whatever that means for you as an individual. It is located between your eyebrows.

A few people have this Chakra open 100 percent, but most people do not. They have learned to put aside their intuition and do not trust this "sixth sense." I work to activate the pineal gland which in turn will activate their intuitive powers. After that the Third Eye will be open. Sometimes it is a learning experience with the Third Eye. It may be open, but trust is not present. I like to tell my clients the percentage to which their Third Eye Chakra is open and encourage them to trust in their intuitive abilities. Some people are afraid of their intuition or do not want to be responsible for what they may "feel" and "know." This is a process in which my clients must learn to love and trust themselves.

The Fifth Chakra – The Throat Chakra

The Fifth Chakra is the Chakra through which you express yourself to the world. Not only do you use it to communicate, but to express your uniqueness and individuality. It is the center for speech and communication as well as your ability to express yourself creatively. The throat Chakra is very powerful because words can transform and create. The throat Chakra is naturally located in the throat area.

Many people have issues with their Throat Chakra due to the variety of ways in which people were killed in past lives. Often when I encounter women who have been abused and hurt in this lifetime, I intuitively feel that they were hung or strangled in past lives. If this has not been addressed or healed, the hurt and fear is brought forward into the current lifetime. It is very difficult for them to speak their Truth if the Throat Chakra is not open. Oftentimes they are afraid to speak up and are very timid. If something is wrong with the

Throat Chakra it will take extra effort on my part to clear out these other past lives, heal the issues, and clear the way for the Throat Chakra to open. It may take two to four weeks for the healing of past lives to take place.

The Fourth Chakra – The Heart Chakra

The Fourth Chakra is the Chakra of love. It is located in the middle of your chest. The ability to feel compassion and forgiveness resides here. It is here that you are able to connect and relate to others and can validate yourself and those around you. You radiate warmth and love to others through this energy wheel.

If you have experienced emotional hurt—and who hasn't?—it is likely that your Heart Chakra is not operating at 100 percent. It is essential that it be opened to allow for love to flow through you and out to others and back to you. It is the place of expression of love of yourself as well as others. If you are in a marriage and your heart is wide open and you have a partner who is operating out of 50 percent of his/her Heart Chakra, it does not feel good. Unless you are able to give love to your children, your grandchildren, others, then often people find themselves in affairs, seeking the love that is missing in their lives in order to make up for what they do not get from their partner.

The Third Chakra – The Solar Plexus Chakra

The Third Chakra has to do with your life energy. It is here where your sense of power, vitality, and inner strength resides. It is from this energy wheel that you have feelings of authority, command, and self-control. It is located right behind the navel.

Whatever your personal power is and however victimized you feel, it will show up in this Chakra. If your Solar Plexus Chakra is not open, or it is spinning at 50 or 60 percent, then you are living out of fear of being controlled or losing control of self. You are not in your power, and you are allowing yourself to be victimized. You are not taking care of yourself. Often, but not always, if you do not feel capable of achieving your desires, the Solar Plexus Chakra will not be open very wide. Your personal power is compromised by how you feel about your body, and you may not feel that you have choice in your life and power.

To get out of the third dimension, you must have the Solar Plexus Chakra spinning at 100 percent. When the third Chakra is open and spinning at 100 percent you have a clear sense of your own power, and you are taking care of yourself. You are in the driver's seat of your life and are not allowing anyone else to control your life.

The Second Chakra ~ The Sacral Chakra

The Second Chakra is all about your relationships—how you connect with others in general but also on an intimate and/or sexual level. You express emotional and sexual needs through this Chakra and it also allows for your ability to respond to others. It is located midway between your navel and the base of your spine. The sacral Chakra affects how you feel about your body sexually.

The Sacral Chakra is about recognizing your sexual energy. It does not have so much to do with being an object of sex but rather as a sexual being. The sexual energy is about feeling good—when you feel good *in* your body, your Sacral Chakra is open. It is the same thing for men and women. There is a shifting taking place because both men and women are beginning to recognize the connection of the Sacral, Heart, and Solar plexus Chakras together. If you do not *feel* like you are sexy, then you will not feel very powerful either.

The First Chakra ~ the Root Chakra

The First Chakra is where the source of primal energy flows in your body. This is the place from which your sense of survival and self-preservation instincts flow. It is located at the base of the spine and gives you a sense of grounded-ness and security. From an energetic standpoint, it is what allows you to live on the physical plane.

The Root Chakra lets you connect to the earth. It is very important, as long as we are in physical bodies, to connect to the earth. We are all one and being all one also includes Mother Earth. She is expecting us to ground our divine energies into her and help her heal just as we heal ourselves. We bring energies from higher levels down into the earth.

I was taught to see a big cord wrapped around my lower spine and imagine that cord go down to the center of the earth, wrap around the very core of the earth, and anchor it there. Some people like to envision the roots of a tree growing deep down into the center of the earth—however you envision your grounding, the point is to anchor yourself there.

Many times when I was young I spent whole days in the woods being ungrounded because I could dream better that way, but that is not the most balanced way to be. I found peace and joy; it was my escape from a very harsh world. However, it is very hard to be in the world if you are not grounded. Some people like not being grounded—they like the feeling of continually being "spacey" and it is fun, but it is impossible to focus if you are not grounded. You help Mother Earth by bringing in higher energies when you stay grounded. You are also part of the earth because as human beings we are all part of one huge ecosystem.

If the lower Chakras are not spinning very well, you are not "in your body" very well. Any energetic connection brings in the power to experience your life, to be a productive part of life. If you remain ungrounded you leave the responsibility for your life to someone else.

Now that you understand the Energy Bodies and their relation to the Chakras, it will be easier to understand the process of clearing out the negative energies that block you from vibrating at a higher frequency.

As I work to open and clear the Chakras, my intention is for the Chakras to be 100 percent open and energetic. I learn so much about a person by checking their Chakras—especially the throat Chakra. It is where we express ourselves, and how we express ourselves tells so much about each and every one of us.

The Process of Clearing

It is apparent to me that when people come to me with sickness (of any sort), it is not the disease itself that is the problem. All disease, however it manifests in the physical realm, always starts in the spiritual realm. The disease is merely an indicator of something that has gone wrong in one or more of the energy bodies. It has just manifested in the physical body. It is the *vibration* that needs attention. It is all about where and how their energy is vibrating. One the spiritual energies are opened and clear, the next step is to deal with the physical dis-ease.

If you only take care of the symptoms and not address the root cause in the spirit, whatever physical symptoms that are being experienced will return. If you come to me or another energy practitioner, you must have to care about yourself; your desire to be healed on the energetic levels must be strong. This process is not about me, it is about *you*. Therefore it is imperative that you realize and want to take responsibility for what you are manifesting in your energy fields.

The first thing that is required is that a person must *want* to be cleared. You may know people who say they want help, but they really do not want to change—preferring their dense existence just as it is. They like to wallow in what is wrong with the world and their own victimhood. *You must allow that person his/her own path in order for you to evolve.* They are afraid of change and not ready. Sometimes life has to get pretty bad for a person to finally be forced to change. They may even consider leaving the planet. It has nothing to do with your path.

Oftentimes a client will refer me to a friend or a family member, but that person is not interested in the healing that I have to offer. I cannot work hard enough to clear them and allow the light of their soul to shine if they are not ready for it or do not want it. I can try and contact their Higher Self and ask for permission to clear, especially if I find this person to be a Lightworker, but ultimately we all have free choice.

The purpose of going through the process of clearing means that the frequency of your vibration is raised and your consciousness is expanded, creating more awareness. This brings in a higher frequency and allows you to connect with your divinity.

A word of caution: the clearing process is not some fun amusement or joy ride that you take on lightly. While you can expect to experience more joy in your life after clearing, it is part of your evolutionary process and you must *want* to go there. Not everyone wants to go at this time.

It Is All about Intention

While it is not essential that a person completely and utterly believe in the work I do, it is essential that they are open to the process and request it. What do you want to take back from this experience? That is the first step to creating intention.

Intention is different from goals. We are taught all our life to set goals. Go to school. Read ten books this summer. Get that diploma. Get that job. Find the right mate. Eat right and be healthy. Make a list of the five things you wish to achieve this year.

Intentions are different. On a very basic level it, we express intention in everything we do. On a broader level, *everything* in life is about intention. What is your intention, what do you hope to achieve for yourself in going to school, reading the books, getting the diploma, having that particular job? What was your intention in picking up this book? What did you intend to happen as you paged through it?

For example, my intention was to write a book in simple understandable terms in order to help those I love (you) prepare for and transition easier into the shift to the fifth dimension. I believe that each person, as well as the planet itself, will soon have this experience.

Intention comes on many levels depending upon where our consciousness is about any particular subject. I intend to write a letter today. I intend to go to work. I intend to drive carefully down the highway. I intend to be a good mother. I intend to serve others. I intend to serve God and honor the God within me. By expressing specific intentions, we start to take in and attract energies for fulfillment

Do you feel the shift in energy within you as you read these intentions? Consider taking parts of your day and setting an intention for everything you do *before* you begin to do it. What do you think would happen to your day? Try focusing on new and higher vibrational intentions instead of focusing on what you had last. *Develop your growth through your intentions.*

Your intention, based on the desire for a particular outcome and the faith in your capacity to have the outcome, is the most powerful tool that exists.

As Dr. Robert V. Gerard says in his book *Change Your DNA, Change Your Life!*

Along with love, intent is the most potent force in the Universe. And the purer the intent the more precise is the manifestation.

My intention is to continually heal my own vessel so that I can hold higher & higher Vibrational energies to help others heal. Since I have started my work, I have physically changed, and anyone who works on healing on a higher level will feel the change within themselves as well. When the life force really flows through you, it leaves you no choice but to go with it.

Keep It Simple

The word I hear more than anything else when I work with people is "blocks." People seem to recognize that they have a lot of blocks and they cannot figure out how to get rid of them.

They say, "I have these blocks and I don't know how to move them. I can't seem to get around these blocks. I've read and read and I've done so many things and I still have these blocks. I've been to this person and to that person and keep doing this and that—but I am still blocked! I am not where I need to be."

People recognize that their energy is blocked because they are awakening to who they truly are and want to find the pathway to get there.

I believe that I am being called to claim my power in order to focus on my work to serve and help others which is so necessary to my life. Part of my mission is to clear out all the blocks and issues that are keeping people from making contact with their higher being and their higher power that reveals who they truly are. Once I can get those blocks out of the way, then it is possible for them to make contact with their Higher Self.

Blocks come from a variety of sources and include outside interference as well as internal interference. They must be removed and cleared.

The Forces of Negativity

Curses

In the Bible a curse was a wish someone put on you so that something bad would befall you. But you do not have to refer to the Bible to understand the power of a curse. Drive down a busy highway and get cut off and what is your immediate reaction? Is it to wish the other driver well? Perhaps it should be, otherwise you have just placed a "curse" on them. In common vernacular it might F—You or Go to H—. These plant negative energies on the other person, and just as you perform these actions, other drivers may be wishing the same on you. In fact, anything you put out rebounds back on you. The transmission of negative energy to another human being constantly connects to your energy as well. You cannot get rid of it. It is embedded and it is living inside your energy. These "curses" must be removed in order for you to be clear. There are also genetic inherent curses such as the belief that you must pay "for your fathers' father's sins."

Implants

Implants are created for manipulation. They are always negative. They are unconsciously implanted in you by others based on control issues another person may have with you. Remember, we use only ten percent of our brain, so a large part of you that is unconscious does things to you. Any piece of you that feels that you are not whole, not complete, you may try to unconsciously take from someone else. The more powerless you feel, the more need you have to take that power from somebody else. The only way to have power is to implant others and take control. It is not possible to do that with love.

Cords

Cords take energy from you. They are not necessarily negative. They can be. They can also be symbiotic. For example, in a husband/wife relationship each person has been bound with cords from the other but there is a give and take. They get positive things from each other, but they give as well. This can happen in other relationships, too.

The cords can become dark when someone else sees him or herself as "less" and you as "more". That person can and may place cords on you in order to feed off your energy. If you have ever had the feeling of being drained after being with someone—as if that person was a "black hole"— sucking all the energy out of you, then you have been corded. Your energy has been compromised.

Whenever there are a lot of black cords and implants on your bodies, the soul is blocked; the light of your soul is blocked from shining. You cannot recognize what you are and you cannot stand in your power. Any darkness not only blocks God's light, it blocks yourself because you are God. When something is blocking your soul, you are blocking the connection to God and the connection to yourself—the God part of you. It is so important that you get completely and totally clear. The soul has to shine through all your energetic bodies so that you know who you are.

The Process

To begin with, there are two ways of looking at light and clearing. You can have a soul that is not 100 percent clear, and you may have pulled in all kinds of negative curses, cords, and implants into the four energetic bodies. Or, you may have a soul 100 percent in the light but that is being blocked by things around the soul and the four energy bodies.

So, you can be 100 percent clear and be in the light 100 percent. You can be 100 percent in the light—your intentions—but not 100 percent clear. You have conscious or unconscious negative patterns and programs on many different levels. Some of these are obtained from past lives, from genetics, or as you go through your present life.

Negative karma can be anything. As like attracts like, what you put out comes back to you. What I strive to do is to eliminate the past, present, and future karma so that you may just live in the present moment.

Science is aware that cellular memory plays an important role in healing. It is possible to allow healing in the body if we can clear that cellular memory because it is that memory in the individual cells that keeps generating the dis-ease. If the cellular memory can be cleared then all the past life, genetics, and this lifetime experiences from the cell, then we can clear disease because that is where it resides.

The more fear energy that can be removed from the planet, the more amplified the heavenly energies can become, the more God energies are able to pervade the planet for healing. It is not possible for me to help you **stay** in the third dimension. I work to get rid of all negative "less-thans" that make up the third dimension. You must let them go or you will keep encountering them over and over again.

The transformation that takes place during the clearing process is not about what is happening around you. It is about what is happening *inside* you. Until we all take that journey within ourselves, nothing that we seek and nothing that we do will be in the fifth dimension.

My personal process in the clearing system includes tuning into my *feeling* so that I *know* and then getting *confirmation* on what I think is true about you. I say prayers to involve our Divine Creator, the Archangels, Ascended Masters, as well as my own team of spiritual guides and healers. They use me as a channel for their divine healing energies to flow through me to clear and dissolve away the dark and negative energies and let the highest light shine. I ask for Archangel Michael's blue flaming sword to cut through and St. Germaine's violet flame to burn and clear all negativity blockages. Then I ask for Golden Creator substance for all healings. As I move forward in the clearing, these requests are repeated over and over during each of the steps outlines below.

A clearing refers to the cleansing and clearing of all genetic issues, the release of energetic blockages consisting of unconscious negative patterns and programs, and the removal of auric attachments and karmic imprints. This allows the healing to take place. Carrying a higher vibration attracts higher vibrating frequencies to you. Long story short: your life becomes easier, better. Clarity increases.

I clear people through their genetic coding—often that brings up struggles which causes them to suffer more. They either suffer mentally or suffer spiritually which will develop into a physical suffering.

I love the people who come to me. I want to convey to them the amount of love I feel for them and the amount of love I feel for God for allowing them to be with me. It is utopia for me to sit in love helping somebody to become clear.

A clearing prepares you to receive the changes required to step into the fifth dimension—one of light and love. A clearing involves cleaning out one's Akashic Records, removing negative implants and cords, and parallel lives in chaos. The purpose of a clearing is to assist, support, and help those on their pathway back to the Divine Creator.

The negative contracts, vows, or agreements that no longer serve you are cleared. They are released.

It is important for me to proceed on a path of service while holding a higher frequency or vibration. This is so that I may help others by shining a brighter light.

What follows is an outline of how I clear the four bodies in my clients and prepare them for the next step in our evolution into the fifth dimension.

Overall the process is one of calling in Protection, encouraging Release, and asking for Healing.

The first thing I do is check to see how much light is in the soul, and that gives me an indication how much work needs to be done to remove any and all blockages.

Then I remove all negative karma, curses, patterns, habits, imprints, and negative programming from each major group: maternal genetic clearing, paternal genetic clearing, and past life genetic clearing.

Next, I remove all negative contracts, vows, and agreements that have ever been made and/or broken. They are erased from the Akashic record books and burned in the Violet flame. All detrimental compassionate connections are removed including all implants and cords.

I remove all negative subconscious programming.

Then I check each of the Chakras to determine how open they are and how well the energy moves through them. I work to open and clear each of the Chakras.

I remove compromising guides, negative, or false guides and replace them with only the highest light guides for that person. I always ask for the highest light when connecting with guides. Then I ask for the highest and best for all concerned.

I remove all parallel, past, and future lives in chaos in order to help my client live in the now.

I remove all negative aspects out of all other world matrixes that are associated with you. I then recode and reintegrate these aspects to create strength and increase consciousness.

I remove all negative or black cords connected anywhere to any energy part of the person.

I remove any dark spirits, negative entities, and Lucifer energies in all aspects and in any dimension.

I clear negative entities from the home and property, sealing all portals.

I heal all wounds and holes in the heart and soul from all lifetimes.

I ask for reintegration of all aspects to come back for wholeness. This will help to create strength and assist in the union of the Authentic Self, which is all that God intended for each of us to be.

I ask for the DNA healing of the Master cell for twelve strands or more, then activation and healing of all cells duplicated and replicated from the master cell. This is completed in a different time frame for each person according to the amount of work already done in this lifetime.

I find the Ascended Masters who want to work with each person and connect that person to those Masters.

I find the Archangels who want to work with each person and connect that person to those Archangels.

Should a client require any special invocations I encourage them to use Joshua David Stone's

Ascension Keys, and I invoke them on behalf of the person.

I dowse any nutrients that may be needed and the amount of benefit of any desire client may have.

Once the energy fields are cleared, it is possible to reconnect to one's self and to others. Once the heart opens, a person can step into the amazing being that she or he was always meant to be.

Detoxification

After a session in which this work is performed on the energy fields, it is very common for people to go through a detoxification process. The symptoms that occur include a wide range of physical, mental, and emotional reactions. Usually they include flu-like symptoms or increased fatigue. But sometimes people have difficulty focusing for a few days or feel like their emotions are very close to their skin and will cry often and easily.

Physical things that can help include making sure of plenty of rest, drinking lots of water, and getting out in the sunshine. It is advisable to stay away from red meat or pork for a few days. Taking a soaking bath with Epsom salts and oil of lavender often helps or an ionic footbath will help to pull the toxins from the body. One person I worked with lost three pounds overnight because of all the implants that were removed!

Look for things that are loved and begin to think from the heart. Once people start to

understand that they are supposed to unconditionally love themselves, the next step is to be
able to love someone else. Once they get over
that hurdle, then they are healed—but it's a big
hurdle for most people. We are not taught to love
ourselves. Somehow we miss the commandment
that the Master gave: Love God, Love your neighbor as yourself. It is the loving yourself first that has
to come *before* loving your neighbor.

It is important to pay attention to the many
acts of synchronicity that may appear, for these
are the phone calls from Spirit. These are the ways
that the Higher Self seeks to help realign with a
person's highest destiny. These can include things
like books that catch one's attention, invitations
that are received in the mail or e-mail, phone calls
from those near and far, and the many opportunities we are all given each day to create a life
of greater lover, more powerful forgiveness, and
higher understanding. These are the Voices of
Spirit operating in life, beneath the outward flow
of events, or even in the midst of them.

Overall, please remember that I do what I can
for you—but you have to do for yourself as well.
The power resides in *you*.

Benefits of Staying Clear

When I perform a clearing process, I intend
that everything be done with ease and grace.
If you can stay clear, then you become more

closely connected and aligned to the Source of All. Your spiritual life expands dramatically and you become more of who you are. Others can sense your improved energy and will want to be around you. With your higher vibrational energies, you have the ability to help others heal themselves.

Some Questions

If I get cleared, can anybody ever take this away from me?

The answer is no, they cannot. You are forever transformed. These are *your* energy fields. As noted above, part of the process is the identification of your spiritual guides and Ascended Masters who stand ready to assist you. You can connect with them and ask for help when you need it.

What is going to happen when I hold more light? Or, what is going to happen when I am healed?

My response is always that you hold more light so that you can be the fullest and complete human being that you are capable of being. The clearer you become, the more effective you will be in loving yourself and serving others. Once you can establish a Divine Connection it is much easier to discover a path of service.

When will I notice a difference?

Almost immediately you will feel lighter, more relaxed within your being. All five of your senses are enhanced. Be prepared for detoxification. It will range from feeling slightly off balance for a day or two to a week in bed with flu-like symptoms, diarrhea, bloating, and headaches. Drink lots of water, rest, avoid eating meat, and get direct sunlight every day. Remember you are transforming.

How will I know I am in the fifth dimension?

You will have let go of fear and judgment of self and others. You will feel peace deep inside that assures you that you are loved and cared for by a powerful Source. You have a knowingness of what feels good for you and act accordingly without hesitation. I feel that here in fifth dimension I am aware that Magic happens daily. That is my desire for you as well.

Will others notice a difference in me?

When you come in contact with others they will unconsciously be aware of your new higher energy frequency and it will feel good for them to be around you. People will be friendlier, want to be in your energy field, and your appearance will be "brighter." It is possible for me see the change in a person after clearing as they appear so much brighter and alive.

Will life be easier?

The Law of attraction is always at work—Like Attracts Like. You always attract people and circumstances that are at your vibrational frequency. Now that this has increased, you will attract others to you with matching higher frequencies. With your intentions set, life starts to flow with less effort on your part. It feels like Magic and good things just show-up.

It may appear that some people are avoiding you. Some people who have a very low frequency will feel their low vibration when around you as they compare themselves to you and will feel uncomfortable and withdraw from your life.

Exercise:

Fear can affect health and well-being. Lack of well-being is not illness; it is a distress of the moment. De-stress yourself in the moment. Once you find yourself in a moment of fear—for whatever reason—take a deep breath and clear your mind of all fear. Keep breathing deeply for a minute or two. Realize that fear is just a reaction to a thought you had. You created the fear.

Choose to think another thought. The mind is so engaged that it involves the entire brain, and that changes the chemistry of the body, the flow of energy, and your entire structure changes!

Make sure you are taking enough of the minerals you need to supplement your body at this time of change.

Affirmation:

I choose to master receiving everything I, the creator, desires—whether I know it or not—that produces the most joy.

I choose to create a loving life, and with each breath I take creative solutions come easily to me.

CHAPTER EIGHT

If you aren't satisfied with the way things are going, realize that you have the powerful ability to observe and perceive reality differently.

Dr. Richard Bartlett

DNA and Why It's Important To Reconnect

In 1953, two young scientists, James Watson and Francis Crick, declared they had "found the secret of life." They discovered the structure of DNA—the chemical that determines the instructions for building and reproducing almost all living things. From a scientific standpoint, it was mindblowing. It made possible the biotechnology industry and it opened the door to the ability to interpret the human genetic blueprint.

The DNA molecule is made up of two chains of nucleotides. The DNA molecule replicates itself during cell division, enabling organisms to reproduce themselves. They are paired in such a way to form the *spiral* of the double helix. Even grade school children today are familiar with this spiral staircase graphic.

We Have More Than Two Strands

Every cell in your body contains DNA. But we actually have twelve strands of DNA. If you were to look at a picture of the double helix, you would easily see that there is a pattern of four repeated three times—over and over and over again. So the DNA structure is base twelve. We were originally created as magnificent and powerful beings of light with twelve active strands of DNA. Eons ago our DNA was split or disconnected. It is because of this that humanity became a fear-based species. The reconnection of the twelve strands is more important than our individual genetic makeup because *with intent* it is possible to change cellular structure.

It has been said that scientists refer to the "junk" DNA present in our genetic blueprint because there appears to be more than we use. It makes you wonder. When you look around our world and see how complex, how beautiful, how multifunctional everything is and how it works in balance with everything else, how can we just write off extra material as "junk?" The Divine Creator did not create any "junk."

When we were disconnected from our other ten DNA strands we could not, without much difficulty, connect to God. Of course, over time Masters appeared who were able to transcend this limitation and connect, but for the rest of us, we were severed from that divine connection and lived in duality. God is unconditional love—the most powerful energy anywhere, anytime. Love is the basis of the energy used to heal. It *is* healing.

Because we have been cut off from that love energy, fear has permeated humankind's consciousness and become the code by which we live our lives. When people come to me I am able to match the love energy to their energy. In this way we can be on the same frequency and their healing becomes possible.

We have twelve strands; we use only two. This causes a limited capacity to use our minds. Ever wonder why people ponder over the fact that we use only 10 percent of our brains? It's because we only have two strands of DNA activated! Now is the time to re-connect the other strands. This will allow us to connect and access higher dimensions of consciousness.

Each person's DNA is different because each person is a different piece of God. The DNA holds light coding, and the twelve strands give us access to twelve levels of spiritual, emotional, physical, and mental awareness and information. Think of your DNA as light encoded filaments—sort of like fiber optics on a very small scale. They carry the Language of Light—the stories of who you are. The number twelve has significance on many levels as well. There are twelve months in the year, twelve heavenly bodies in the solar system, twelve hours of darkness, and twelve hours of light. There were twelve apostles. It is possible for us to access that information on all of those levels instead of just the two levels available from the two strands of DNA commonly accepted as reality. However, these strands are not chemical and therefore cannot be seen.

We are oscillating, vibrating beings of light.

As Dr. Richard Bartlett puts so succinctly in his book, *Matrix Energetics,* here's the bottom line at our base level as a physical being:

We are composed of light and information,
or consciousness.

In that light is recorded our whole life including genetic codes as well as previous life times.

One of the first things I do in my clearing is ask that the Master cell, the first cell, be healed and all twelve strands be put back together as God intended. Then I ask each replication of that Master cell be replicated and duplicated—that all twelve strands be activated until every cell in the body has all twelve strands.

This starts after the clearing work is completely healed. Then the DNA will begin to replicate. It takes time for the cells to duplicate themselves after the master cell - part of the detoxification process. It might take a little longer if the person carries the burden of an inordinate amount of responsibility in her or his life. The intention is always that the person be healed for the highest good.

Why DNA Reconnection?

When your DNA is reconnected, your vibrational frequency rises. As you clear out the lower energy blockages—the curses, implants, cords, and all the negative energies—you are then able to "download" higher consciousness from your Higher Self and raise your vibration.

The goal is to become *conscious* creators. When we no longer create by default, there is no reason to look around at the events and circumstance of our life and ask, "How did that happen?" Instead, we can step into our power and realize, "I created that!" If we don't like it, then we can simply create something different. Our universe can and will rearrange itself to accommodate the pictures of reality we desire. Through the reconnection of our DNA, it will be possible to bring in information and light to change our world and heal our planet as we are able to hold higher frequencies.

In the third dimension, your physical body is very important because it controls the frequency you can attract and hold from your Higher Self. Your body is an essential part of who you are because of this. You cannot master the third dimension without getting your four bodies in alignment with these higher frequencies. By re-connecting your DNA, you can then hold those higher frequencies and thus progress into those higher levels of consciousness.

What is a Miracle?

A "miracle" is merely the ability to create matter out of consciousness. Since you can create your own reality, it only makes sense that miracles are possible.

Going back to what I said at the beginning about thought and consciousness, the way "miracles" are created begins with your intent. There are people on the earth today who can do this—create matter out of consciousness. I am not just talking about creating the parking space by the front door of the grocery store, either. (If you have "played" at all with creating your own reality, you should be able to do that easily.) Instead, I am referring to the "miracles" of healing that take place on many levels, the ability to turn around events in your life through the power of your intent and consciousness—the capacity to transmute energy into form. You begin to know that you posses the ability to create abundance, prosperity, health, wonderful relationships, peace, love, and rock n' roll.

As energy beings we are constantly moving and evolving. When you begin to see who you really are and you start to understand that spiritual component, that Source energy, within you, *you change* and *you create change*. Simply put, when you re-connect the twelve strands of DNA, you begin to create your own reality. In time the reality you create can be considered by others miraculous, but it can become your new normal.

Manifestation must align with our Soul contract since all of the power from the twelve DNA strands will be found when those contracts are fulfilled. Once you have re-connected, those soul contracts become more apparent to you. You are inspired to act in ways that you might have thought about before but now you are *compelled* to do so. In learning to love yourself you only want the very best for yourself.

When you are re-connected and love is the basis of your motivation, it becomes easier and easier to manifest what you want. In order to master the third and fourth dimensions, you must master your ability to create that reality through your thoughts and emotions.

That is what it is all about—being able to move past whatever is holding you back and become a greater you. Your DNA—your genetic DNA—may have caused you to re-do things that your father did, your grandfather did, your grandmother did—the good things as well as the not-so-good things.

I once cleared and re-connected a woman's DNA whose great grandfather was a Native American Cherokee who had walked the Trail of Tears. It was an incredible release for her. She had carried the genetic coding of all that pain with her until it was finally cleared.

Benefits to Reconnecting Your DNA

When your DNA is reconnected it is possible to step into the power of who you truly are. It allows you to process into the fourth dimension of consciousness and prepares you for the fifth. Because fear and guilt are released, you can accept full responsibility for the outcome of your life—whatever successes you experience. Once you know that you can trust the Universe, you give more energy to your intentions which allows surrender to your highest good. You know that you may not always know how your highest good is manifested, but the Universe and the Divine Creator know. Therefore, it is possible to have a greater sense of freedom.

When your DNA has been reconnected it is possible to feel more strongly the emotions of joy and love. Whatever has been going on in your life can be resolved with peace and calmness while allowing you to detach from the "drama" in your life and in the lives of others around you. Many people experience an increase in general vitality, confidence, and security once their DNA has been reconnected. With almost all of my clients there has been a deep emotional release which has allowed for physical, emotional, mental, and spiritual healings. They tell me that they are better able to discern the essence of situations and events in their lives by the experience of increased clarity and detachment from the outcome.

Self-Expression

Because DNA reconnection helps to open and allow the throat Chakra to spin more efficiently, it becomes easier to speak the truth of who you are. Many people have been reticent to act from the heart of that which they know and feel themselves to be. They have sublimated their truth and the expression of it. This has been a particular problem for baby boom women and those who are older. This is the last generation of women who have sublimated their truth so that they could support the men in their life. Once DNA has been reconnected they often find themselves no longer afraid to speak their mind and to honor their own feelings. DNA reconnection facilitates the opening of the Chakras and the beginning of a confident expression of a more satisfying life of personal power.

Recognition of Your Life Purpose

It is possible after reconnection to become aware of why you have chosen to be here at this time. When past life issues have been resolved in the clearing of all negative blocks it is possible to see what exactly it is that you are here to achieve. You become more conscious of what your soul needs to bring in joy and bliss into your life.

The soul wants more than anything to feel this and know it is satisfied with direction and intention of the work you are doing. You become aware of the deep longing when listening to the soul. As you listen and feel from the heart you attract greater and greater joy into your life. You also become more aware of synchronicity and the power that has to guide and lead you into the direction of your purpose.

You may recognize many skills you have learned along your life path are useful now in your purpose. People start to show up who want to tell you or show you something that you become excited about. You can almost feel your soul taking flight with joy of hearing what they have to say. Perhaps a knowing comes to you that this is something you can do or even something you feel you have done in a past life. It all feels so good and so right to you.

Dreaming

Many people experience lucid dreaming after their DNA has been reconnected. Lucid dreaming is dreaming in a state in which you *know* that you are dreaming. In this type of dreaming, you feel as if you are fully awake and recognize that you have the power to change the events in the dream. It is a remarkable way to be able to dream and to increase your understanding of the power within you.

You are also able to better facilitate dream interpretation. As dreams most often unfold symbolically, the symbols and what they represent in your dreams are now more discernable. Dreams may represent issues in your life that are unresolved. Many people have the same dreams over and over for this reason—they are unable to understand or face certain issues. After DNA reconnection it is possible to be able to understand the significance and symbolic nature of dreams as well as to decipher the meanings and therefore deal with the issues.

It is possible for you to program your dreams by setting an intention before your dream? Do you need assistance on solving a work or personal problem? Do you need a healing? You can release limiting beliefs if you ask for assistance and clarity in your dreams. Merely state your intention just prior to falling asleep. It is also advisable to set an intention to remember your dreams so that you can make the best use of that guidance.

Higher Frequency

Once the twelve strands have been reconnected, it becomes possible to do the major genetic energy clearing referred to in the previous chapter. These take place on both the maternal and paternal lineages as well as in the past lives you have lived. In performing the cleansing, the patterns and programs that no longer serve you are removed.

DNA reconnection clears, balances, and aligns your four energy bodies (mental, physical, emotional, and spiritual). It allows you to raise your vibration and integrate these four bodies so that you are able to hold a greater light frequency.

Since you are now holding a higher frequency and align to the Divine Creator, you are able to better connect with certain Ascended Masters and Archangels. Every person has spirit guides and when reconnected, you can ensure that your guides are there for you in your highest good. You can ask for assistance based upon your highest and best purpose and become open to receiving guidance and instruction from them in this process.

Once open to the reconnection you may have more of a sense of the thrill of just being alive. The internal change that overcomes the physical being dramatically expands the stamina of the life force that flows through you when all levels of DNA are reconnected.

Altering Your Blueprint

Once you are reconnected to the twelve strands of your DNA, your personal world and power change dramatically. When you are aligned with creator Truth you will have access to the best information available. You can identify with whatever it is you want to create, become it, and live it as though it had already happened and thus manifest it in the physical world.

As your twelve completely healed and evolved helixes inside each cell of your body are activated, your full brain capacity is also activated. You can release fear and guilt. You can make decisions that were previously not possible. You are able to accept full responsibility for everything that happens in your life as you have created it. You are able to fully live in the present.

DNA recoding helps us to hook up with all of our higher abilities—intuition, telepathy, the deeper knowing of our connection to Source energy. We are now able to better connect with and communicate with that energy. Our lives take on a higher level and a greater significance.

It is best to begin to ask for spiritual growth, to *intend* spiritual growth. Know that you now have the power to alter your energy blueprint through thought and feeling so that you can change anything in your physical experience.

Exercise:

Ask your Higher Self, "Show me your truth regarding *(whatever issue that may have your attention)* so that I can manifest that more in my life."

Fill in the blanks:

I know my greatest desire is to

Be _____

See _____

Feel _____

Hear the words _____

Affirmation:

I am connected and loved by the Divine Creator.

I am never alone.

Great light and love from the Divine Creator flows through me.

CHAPTER NINE

We can never obtain peace in the outer world
until we make peace with ourselves.
His Holiness, the Dali Lama

The Daily Practice

Throughout this book I have suggested exercises and affirmation to help you to become your authentic self. It is very important for you to stay in alignment with who you truly are. To help you do so I suggest a daily practice. This does not require a lot of time—just a few minutes during the course of your regular day. Make your spirituality a practical discipline. The benefits are immeasurable in your preparation for what is about to happen.

On the most basic level of our bodies—the subatomic level—we are composed of light—photons. It is the light in our bodies that will be expanding. In order to prepare for our bodies to hold more light, we must allow for a change in the way we look at ourselves and our world. The best way to do that is to perform a daily practice. This practice can be anything you want it to be that makes you feel good and expands the amount of love you can feel and hold. You can design your own daily practice in any way you choose.

The purpose of the daily practice is to be good to yourself. To love yourself.

Below is a list of practices that you may wish to use. They are only a suggestion, a guideline that may or may not work for you. You may find in trying some of these suggestions that you will use some and discard others. You may find in other methodologies that work better for you. Feel free to edit, alter, add, or delete any of the suggestions. I suggest you continue to read, research, find, and do whatever feels good to you.

Begin a Practice Today

Awake each morning and say, "Today I will trust and allow that all is working in Divine Order for the highest and best for me."

Meditate

Diana Robinson said, *"Prayer is when you talk to God; meditation is when you listen to God."*

I advocate both forms of communication but begin your day by listening. Meditation can take a variety of forms, depending upon what feels good to you. Some people like to spend a certain amount of time just sitting quietly, calming their minds and going into an altered state. If this feels good to you and you have not meditated before, start slowly—only five minutes a day. You can increase the time over the course of the days you meditate. The biggest challenge to meditating is quieting the inner chatter of your mind. If you have never tried to meditate before and you attempt to start out at half an hour or longer you will get very frustrated and quit. The mind does not like to be quiet.

The basic method of meditation is to get into a place where you can comfortably relax in a sitting position—someplace where you will not be disturbed for the duration of the time you wish to be in meditation. Sit with your spine straight and your feet flat on the floor. Take three deep, slow breaths.

Breathe. Listen. Feel your heartbeat. See if you can slow down and just BE. Clear your mind of all thought. Just let it go. Every time a thought comes to you, think of encasing it in a balloon (like a cartoon character) and let it float off into space. Do not judge or entertain your thoughts, just let them go.

Some people find that guided meditation is the most helpful to them. There are plenty of practitioners who offer recorded versions of meditations. Sometimes it helps to play music that puts you into an altered state. Steven Halpern is a musician known for his soothing music written for healing, massage, sleep, and meditation. His *Chakra Suite* is particularly helpful for opening up the Chakras.

Still others find that it is not possible to find that altered state of meditation unless they are exercising. Once you get your body going in repetitious movement, you mind has a tendency to expand and move into that quiet space within. So if it feels better to you, go for a walk, a swim, or a bike ride—whatever creates movement that you do not have to think about and as long as you are in a safe place and can let yourself get into that altered space.

Action Choices

Move your body. Go for a walk, join an exercise club, hire a personal trainer. Whatever feels right to you. Your body is a temple of all that is holy within you. When something goes wrong it manifests there as an indicator of what you are thinking/feeling where the blockage is. Part of loving yourself is loving your body. It is the vehicle that will take you to the fifth dimension.

For many years I have practiced the Five Rites outlined in Peter Kelder's slim volume entitled *The Ancient Secret of the Fountain of Youth*. I found this book after I had experienced severe back pain that was not relieved through chiropractic adjustment. I needed a way to release the pain, and one day a flyer for this book landed in my mailbox. It was one of the significant synchronicities of my life. I began to do the exercises, and it relieved the pain. I have not had problems with my back since. In the past seventeen years I have practiced these rites daily and only miss a day or two per year. It is easily obtainable online or in a library.

The rites are basically five yoga exercises that are not complicated but work in combination to open the Chakras and get the vortexes of energy spinning in your body. Testimonials from the thousands of people who have practiced these "rites" over the years verify that they do work to make dramatic improvements in the flexibility and youth of your body.

What You Eat

Your body needs nourishment. Especially in this time of the change in consciousness we all need to pay attention to what we ingest into our bodies. Increase the amount of mineral supplements at this time because your body is changing physically.

Eons ago, before we fell from the Light, we lived in harmony with all living things. We did not eat the meat of the animals who were our friends. There was plenty of food for all that came from the abundance of the earth. The eating of meat was a mutation. Therefore, I encourage you to forgo the eating of any meat. If this is not possible for you, I would advise that you only eat free-grazing animals and that you take up or return to the blessing of your food each and every time before you eat.

Fear resides in the tissues of our bodies. The way animals are kept and then processed for their meat is fear-based. That fear resides in the tissues of the animals you eat and therefore is there when you ingest meat. Always bless your food before you eat; this will help to release the toxins of that fear. Be thankful to the animal that has sacrificed its life to energize yours.

In addition, always bless the liquids that you drink. Perhaps you are familiar with the work of Dr. Masaru Emoto. He discovered the impact of thought and intent on water. Dr. Emoto took water samples from around the world, slowly froze them, and then photographed them with a dark field microscope with photographic capability. Each water crystal is unique. The crystals with negative thought and intent were disjointed and dark. The ones with positive thought and intent were perfectly formed and quite beautiful. Since our bodies are comprised mostly of water, we need to be aware of the intentions we put into the water that we put into our bodies. Therefore, I always recommend blessing the water you drink, expressing appreciation for all the good things that it will do for your body.

Do Something for Mother Earth

If you do not already recycle, start now. An aluminum can takes five hundred years to decompose—plastic is with us forever. On the show *Northern Exposure*, which was popular some years ago, a reference to recycling the character named Adam made has always stayed with me.

The line he said was something like this: "The ancients left the pyramids; we are leaving piles of garbage for generations to come." There is so much truth in that. Stop polluting Mother Earth, her oceans and gardens. So much of what we use can be transformed and used again.

Do Something for Others

Depending upon which of the kingdoms you lean toward you might wish to include an aspect of that kingdom. Do what you love in preparation to be all the love you are.

If you are an animal lover, then spend time every day with the animal that you have. If you have a dog, sit down and pet the dog, feel the unconditional love flow back and forth between the two of you. Particularly if you feel any anxiety, this is an excellent way to lower blood pressure. If you feel any anxiety about an issue in your life, it can be soothed in those few minutes you spend stroking the fur of your favorite canine.

If you are a gardener, or if you simply enjoy a garden, go and walk or sit in one. Look around you at the plants and their individual perfection. Notice how exquisite and unique each one is in comparison to another—how vibrant the colors. Lose yourself in the appreciation of variety and combination. If you have access to a public garden, spend some time in that garden and know that it has been created just for your enjoyment.

Breathe in the same air the plants do. Smell the fragrance. Or go for a short walk in your neighborhood and just look at the trees. Really look at them. Recognize how magnificent they are. Notice the different plantings in the homes in your area—flower boxes, bushes, even what the grass looks like. Begin to notice what is important to you in the yards in your neighborhood and how do you feel when you recognize and admire them?

If you are drawn to the kingdom of the angels, spend some time with them. Go to a quiet place— it might be a garden or a church or a sitting room in a library. Open your mind to receive their messages and assistance.

If you are drawn to the kingdom of humanity there is no better way than to connect to others than to joyfully serve. Pick a non-profit that speaks to you and volunteer your time. There are hundreds of opportunities available in your own community, no matter how small or how big, that run the gamut of anything and everything that you could possibly have interest in. Find an organization whose mission resonates with you and whose work makes your soul happy. Is it working with the homeless? Seniors? Children? Is it volunteering at your church to serve refreshments after service or be on a committee? Every single person has strengths and skills that can be utilized. Choose someplace that resonates with you. Give a small portion of your time on a regular basis and it will open your heart and your world to others. It will allow you to be of service on the highest level.

Sometimes your interest and love can be combined. For example, volunteering to help clean up a riverbank fulfills your love of nature AND assists humanity.

Read or Listen to Audio Recordings

Integrate what you have learned into your daily experience. Read one chapter from a book that propels you on your journey to the fifth dimension. There are now so many out there that give you differing perspectives on what is going on and how to step into the spiritual being you inherently are. Read at least one chapter from a book each day. With access to so much information it is very easy to do this—you can even do it online!

If you are not the type of person who likes to read, get or download an audio book. Many people like to hear the words of an author spoken by the author herself or himself. It is possible today to get just about any book this way.

Prayer

End your day by talking with God through prayer. Always remember that power resides within you. Invoke assistance for the particular things you desire from the higher beings, angels, and ascended masters who are here to assist you in your journey and to manifest those desires.

Many disciplines encourage you to create your own altar space in your home utilizing representations of earth, fire, water, and air. This could be a table or shelf where you put anything that resonates with you on a spiritual level. It can include candles, books, feathers, statues, crystals—whatever you would like.

You can orient yourself to the seven sacred directions as part of your process of prayer. Face east with your back to the west, north to your left, south to your right. The sky is up, the earth is down, and the center is in your heart. Place your focus in each direction in that order and honor that space. Speak a prayer of gratitude and thanksgiving for all that comes to you from every direction.

In chapter twelve I have included a prayer from Patricia Cota-Robles that you may wish to use as a prayer or invocation and incorporate into your daily practice.

Exercise:

Before you go to bed always review the events of the day from the perspective of how much you appreciated and enjoyed the ways in which they unfolded. Say prayers of appreciation for the care and assistance you received through the day. Give thanks to the Divine Order of your life for the next day.

Affirmations:

Every day I appreciate the manifestation of Divine Order in my life.

My life is magical.

My desires manifest for the highest good of all.

I find my divine bliss each day.

My life flows with ease and grace.

CHAPTER TEN

We achieved galactic synchronization in
1987, galactic resonance in 1998,
and we will be offered galactic citizenship in 2012—provided that
by this time we have attained multidimensional
consciousness as a species.

Barbara Hand Clow

No Child Left Behind

We are all children of the Living God. We are all sparks of the Divine Light of the Divine Creator. Someday, eons from now, each and everyone one of us will return and merge once again with The All of which we are only a very small part. We will truly become One.

Until then, we are on our individual right and perfect path, expanding the Universe with every thought, emotion, and action. We can't make a wrong choice; we will never finish the work. Expansion just keeps on expanding through us. Each child born into the world is part of that expansion and has the benefit of all that has come before.

It does not matter what your religion is, or even if you have no religion at all. All paths are viable; all paths lead to the same place—the perfect expansion of the Universe, the perfect reunion with All That Is.

Just as you choose to awaken, the path you choose is also a choice. You are never without freewill. We all came here at this time in order to help create this Shift—to assist in the transition to the fifth dimension. You may or may not be aware of what your part is in this, but it is now time to wake up and think about it.

We are all here to evolve together. We *volunteered* to be here. We *wanted* to be here when the world shifted from darkness, ignorance, and fear into light, humanity, and love.

We are the Lightworkers, and it is our mission to show the way—so many have already. Now we take it to mass consciousness so that no child is left behind. We must all be given the opportunity to move into the fifth dimension of consciousness.

The Call of Soul

Your soul is calling to you. Learn to listen. Your soul only wants the very best for you, and by listening to your soul you receive guidance and experience peak moments of joy. When I learned to listen to my soul, I found peak moments of joy that I might have missed otherwise. I took a deep breath and welcomed my authentic self. My mind had never really given me those awesome moments of Love and Bliss, but boy my soul has! My soul knows that now is the time that I have trained for all my life. This work I do allows the love of Divine Creator to flow through me to connect with another, in assisting them to become all that they were created to be.

Now is the time to learn to love who you are and notice what you LOVE to do. Now is the time to discover what gives your soul great joy and to trust this feeling. Now is the time to sit in the silence and let your soul imagine, and then write it down.

The fifth dimension is ruled by the heart and guided by the right brain. When your left brain tries to take over and rule you with doubt and fear, allow your soul to speak to you so that you can move into love.

Ascension

To ascend means to move up in some form.

Ascension is a word that is used to describe the process that will begin at the end of 2012. It refers to the change in frequency of Earth's electromagnetic field, of our very cells and in the focus of our consciousness. It heralds the influx of love on the planet.

Therefore, to ascend means that the vibrations of the soul and the physical body that contains the soul increase until both of them are able to reach a higher plane of existence. Part of that process is the shift in consciousness. It is the movement from the dense reality of the third dimension to the fifth dimension—one of light and love and wholeness.

Organically speaking, the cells in our body will change from a carbon-based structure to a crystalline structure. We will be able to hold more light in a way that has not been available to humanity since the time of Atlantis. We will be able to vibrate at a higher level. Because our cells will be able to take in more light, there will be more space in between them to allow for that light. You will no longer need to die or leave your physical body. All that needs to be done is to simply change the vibrational role of your physical being and take your body with you.

You can rearrange the molecular structure by allowing in more light. I believe some, a very few, will actually burst into light bodies—their form will still be visible, but they will hold little density. It all depends upon the level or strata of the fifth dimension that one ascends to at the time.

This is not really as unusual as it seems. Did not the prophet Elijah do this in the Old Testament? What about Jesus after the resurrection and his *ascension* into Heaven? And his mother, Mary? Her ascension is noted as well. In 2012 this will be a reality available to everyone. We are moving very quickly into the next step of our evolution, and it is not going to take millions or thousands of years. It is going to happen in the very near future.

We ascend.

What is that going to look like? The Bible refers to the Rapture. In some ways, I believe this is another word for Ascension—it is just not going to look like most people expect it to look like. There will be no division into believers and nonbelievers—we all have the opportunity to ascend. The Divine Creator's love is unconditional. Ascension cannot be looked upon as a product. It is a personal transition in the heart. Everyone will experience it differently based upon soul growth and experience.

What is important in life right now is how much you love yourself and others. How much you are willing to assist and help other people? How much do you allow, surrender, and trust your Divine Creator to guide you? It is not required that you become Mother Theresa—there was only one—but you can demonstrate it right where you are. Volunteer and start to serve even in small ways. It is so important that you have opened your heart Chakra so that you are able to receive love and give love freely.

With all the turmoil in the earth that has taken place—earthquakes in Haiti, Chile, and Japan, volcanoes, floods, and tsunamis taking a huge toll on humanity—these are opportunities for all of us to open our hearts to one another. How we stand together, what we offer to one another is our future.

Your power is in the present moment. You can exhibit that power for love in your daily activities as long as they are aligned with the Divine Creator. Accept that challenge and step into who you are today. Allow others to feel your frequency so that your energy can help teach them how they want to feel. This is showing them the way.

Ascend with Intention

I have underlined the purpose intention plays in everything you do. The ascension process is no exception. If your intention is to expand, to grow spiritually, to love, then your ascension will allow the soul to consciously move back and forth between dimensional levels. Think of the joy you experience in remembering all the information the soul has gathered through each and every one of your incarnations. Know that you have access to all the truths that were learned from your many soul journeys. That has been shut down through fear and control in the third dimensional reality, but soon all that will be gone and you will remember.

Everyone Is Going

In 2002 it became clear to me that *all* souls are going to step into the fifth dimension. They may not be on the same schedule, but everyone is going and no one is going to be left behind. We all, each and every one of us, are on the verge of Enlightenment. It is not going to take years to achieve; you will not have to work really hard to achieve it. Every person on the planet is going as well as the planet itself. It is going to be a gigantic leap into the fifth dimension, so hold onto your hat because it is going to be an unbelievable ride.

This is our moment. In the deepest recesses of our hearts we have always known that these times would come. It is not the end. It is the beginning. We are all eternal beings. There is no death.

Holding a third-dimensional reality on the earth has been a drag on the entire Universe. We are all evolving to God—no matter what vibration we currently hold, no matter what planet we maintain our consciousness on, no matter what form our body may take. We are all connected and because of that those of us living in the third dimension are holding back others in those dimensions and realities from moving forward in their evolution. So much attention is being given to the earth right now because of what we are about to experience.

Recognize that we are all evolving—all souls on all planets and all universes are evolving. Our journey is ultimately about evolving back to the Divine Creator. It is important for each and every one of us to do the work that each soul has to do in order to achieve that.

As we are being cleared and our DNA is reconnected in preparation for this most important evolution, we let go of all those things that no longer serve us. This is the baggage that we will not be able to take into the next step. Somewhat like starting a new relationship—you cannot take the baggage of the old relationship with you as it will not serve the new relationship. So it is with this evolution process. You cannot take the baggage of hate, of despair, of lack, of mistrust, of ugliness with you. You must release it all.

Lower frequencies of duality, such as fear and limitation, cannot exist on the fifth dimension of consciousness because it is based on complete and unconditional love. And you recognize that you are truly ONE.

Right now, right here, we are living in an important time when the expansion of the Universe will take a quantum leap as we move from a third dimension of density to the fifth dimension of light.

The Earth Is Going

The earth is a living being. As we were created by God, so was she. We are connected to the earth and she is to us. If more people "got that" we would treat her with much more respect and not take her for granted. This wonderful planet is a jewel in the universe. As Chief Seattle said so long ago, "Earth does not belong to us; we belong to earth."

Listen to the news for only a moment (not that I recommend even a moment of it), and you will hear all about the disasters taking place around the world—the earthquakes, flooding, fires. If you saw the pictures of people trying to breathe the smoke-filled air in Moscow in 2010 or the overwhelming videos of the earthquake and tsunami in Japan in 2011, you have some sense of how everyone is affected by what is going on in nature.

Right now the earth is spinning differently on her axis—the earthquake in Chile had an impact upon that—and so she occupies a new space in the cosmos. Just as we are preparing our bodies to hold more light, so is our dear planet. Expect more weather pattern changes, wildfires, flooding, volcanic eruptions. The purpose of this is to create a clearing of the earth's energies. Those who do not wish to go along with the ascension process may choose to leave through the various disasters that are being created in the cleansing process. Just as our lives are being rocked by economic, physical, spiritual forces, so it is for the earth.

So the entire physical planet is ascending. It is the most exciting thing that ever happened on earth, and it will happen very soon—in our lifetime. And, because we are all connected, the entire Universe is holding its breath waiting for us to embrace the Shift that is coming. Other planets are on the brink of ascension. If we go—Earth, then they can continue evolving on their paths as well. The Earth will ascend and as its inhabitants, we will remain in alignment with her and ascend as well.

If any of this information resonates with you then you know that your DNA has been activated and more light is pouring into your cells. You are decoding the information coming in through the light that is bombarding the planet in terms of cosmic rays and recognizing how your life is being altered. There will come a time after we move into the fifth dimension in which the third dimension will cease to exist as we know it. We will ask ourselves, "What was the third dimension like?" because we will not remember a time that was not based upon love.

Whether or not you go with the ascension is up to you. Some will move up to the higher vibrational plane, others may begin a new cycle at the present third-dimensional density on a physical level somewhere else in the universe. It reminds me of a *Star Trek Second Generation* episode called "Homeward." A planet was going to be destroyed and one of the main characters circumvented the Federation's *Prime Directive* by beaming an entire village aboard the Enterprise and placing them in the holodeck which recreated their village. Then they were beamed down onto a new planet very similar to the old without any of the inhabitants knowing the difference! If you choose not to ascend, your next experience may be something very like that episode.

Your Frequency

Once you can consistently maintain a stable frequency—not the roller coaster of emotions up and down—you can obtain what you desire. The way to do that is to act as if you are divinely guided in every decision you make. Believe that you are in the right time and the right place. Know that everything is orchestrated for your higher good, your higher evolution, and surrender to this higher good. Just allow.

Can you get to the point where you love yourself as God loves you? What if you could hold yourself as your own newborn child and allow the love and adoration for your self to flow through you, and know that you will do the very best for yourself?

Begin to set an intention each day to go through your life with an experience of more clarity. What makes you feel joy and connected and alive? Ask how you can allow more happiness in your life.

Exercise:

Start now right where you are. Observe and assist those around you in line at the grocery store, your child's teacher, the client or co-worker who just rubs you the wrong way— your spouse or significant other. Begin just by concentrating on the positive aspects of that person, event, or situation. No matter what, strive to demonstrate unconditional love.

Affirmation:

I am allowing my higher good in every moment.

Everyone and every thing is a vessel for my good to come to me.

CHAPTER ELEVEN

You, yourself, as much as anybody in the entire universe,
deserve your love and affection.

Buddha

When Love Is The New Currency, How Rich Will You Be?

A tremendous spiritual awakening is taking place right now. It is like waking up from sleep—it is a gradual flow into consciousness. This journey is taking place for hundreds of thousands of people on the planet every day. Perhaps you are one of them or you are helping someone else to awaken. Each person is on his/her own perfect path and travels it in the unique expression of the divine that he or she is.

Change is in the air. And in the water. And in Mother Earth. We are living in an extraordinary time of change, unseen by any living human before. The ancients tell us we are at the end of days—a time when we will experience transformation so profound that it will affect even our DNA. A time when we will shift into a new sense of time, a new sense and state of being. As this is written, there is a profound awareness that time is speeding up, moving us faster and faster, irrevocably toward that change. Right now our social, economic, political, and religious foundations are shifting and moving, somewhat like the earth when the continents moved into the alignment which we know them to be in today.

Throughout my life it t has always been my intention in my work to lift people up. It is what I live for. In my work I am privileged to sit down on a one-to-one basis with people and allow them to be in my energy. And they allow me to be in their energy. It is a tremendous opportunity for healing on both sides of the table. And for me, it is euphoric because in my work I am living the bliss of my purpose. I get to connect with the Divine Creator but I also get to connect with the divine within each and every person with whom I interact. I get to meet the Divine Creator energy that resides in each person and offer guidance on how she or he can engage with her or his own higher energy.

Commencement

When you graduate from school you participate in a commencement exercise. While most people think this means the end of a period of time, it actually encompasses the beginning. So it is with this chapter; so it is with you. Spiritual growth should not be difficult. It is who you are. Allow it. Be it. Start now.

All my life I have felt so different from everyone else. I have tried not to be that different. I have tried to hide who I am. I no longer have to hide. Perhaps you have felt this way as well. Perhaps you have felt as if you were the odd person in your family or group. There is no better time than now to honor that "difference" in you. Step into who you truly are and, believe me, you will make a difference in your family, your community, your country, our world.

There is still a great deal of work to do. I ask that you hold the light and love of God with me at the highest state of consciousness where you are right now. Wherever you are and whenever you can, envision the planet bathed in this light as well as every single person who resides upon it.

There is a limitless supply of love energy from God. Releasing fear is a big job in itself. We are so connected to that fear in so many places. The media feeds our fear about warning us about all the awful events that have taken place today. The "reality" shows on television often invite us to believe the worst of people instead of the very best. Disconnecting from fear is the biggest thing we can do for ourselves. Fear is an illusion. It only exists because you had a third-dimensional reaction to the condition. Begin to choose how you react and you move into the fourth dimension.

Have you been brought up in pain? Then you have cut yourself off from feeling. It has been easier not to feel. This is a major block to allowing love into your life. Release the resistance of the fear of not loving or being loved enough and let go of blocks. Work toward loving yourself but if even that is difficult for you, begin by loving something *about* yourself—even if it is only the color of your eyes. You must love in order to heal. My healing work and loving work are wide open.

Know that the energies of love exist. Look for them wherever you can find them—in the smile of someone you know, in nature, or in the unconditional love of your pet. Once you recognize that, once you can start somewhere, it is like a ladder or stepping stone to connect to that. You can connect to something higher and keep moving up. It is all about moving forward in love.

Open Your Heart

What are you compelled to do from your heart?

So much has happened in the world—the floods, earthquakes, tsunamis. As awful as they have been and as difficult for those who have had to live through them, they have been opportunities for all of us in the world to open our hearts to one another.

When one other person shifts, then you can feel it. When you shift, you change and the world around you changes.

Those of you who are aware that you have a sacred mission—it could be helping one other person or millions of others—you will feel the pull of it.

Trust yourself, take a step, just one step at a time on the golden pathway. You are being pulled to be bigger than you are. It is not about the ego; it is about your soul mission—that is bliss and joy. Recognize that you are in bliss and joy. When it doesn't feel good, you are in ego and you have to stop.

You chose to be here at this time and you were chosen to be here at this time. There is no need to fear; everything is unfolding in divine order. Look for the miracles that are happening every day that lead to the opening of hearts all over the world. The emotion of love is the key to ascension. With love figure out the multidimensional nature of yourself, learn to heal it, and through that become connected to every other person on the planet.

When we refer to the Heart of anything, what do we mean?

- The Heart of the matter
- Heart of the city
- Heart of the building
- Heart of the organization
- Heart of the country
- Heart of the family

Sometimes the heart is a person, sometimes it is an idea, and sometimes it is a symbol.

What do you believe is the heart of America?

Overall, whatever the heart is, it is a feeling and it comes from the sacred flame that is lit in the heart itself. We are the heart of the world, and we must act and feel like it in order to advance into the next platform of evolution of our species and it must be love.

Balance

We are moving into a state of balance between the masculine and feminine. Do not think of those terms in relation to sexuality or the purely physical sense because it means something different spiritually. In the spiritual sense the feminine represents the creative, open, fluid part of you—the part of you that gets those great ideas on every level for every facet of your life. The masculine part is the part that acts on those ideas. These two elements work exceptionally well together when in balance.

For eons, we have been out of balance. The feminine has been sublimated to the masculine. The feminine energy shut down the throat Chakra energy and stifled speaking truth in deference to masculine energy. In the patriarchal societies throughout our history, intuition was downplayed and ridiculed. Action was king. This resulted in the energy of the heart Chakra being sublimated to the energy of the solar plexus Chakra and the exercise of power.

However, all that is changing now. We move into a time when both aspects will be recognized and honored equally. The feminine will speak, and the masculine will feel.

Think about your own experience—has this imbalance proved true in your relationships? Is it still true? Are you beginning to speak your truth or to feel the emotions of your heart?

So many women during the past thirty years have stepped into power and become a force in the world and on many levels. What are their role modes? There are no powerful female gods— they are traditionally male. Many women have taken the male power role models as our own. We have to create our own models—look for the best and emulate that. There has to be stabilization. We must create the empowered feminine; the Goddess must return.

The reintegration of all aspects of who you are marks you as ready to come back into wholeness. This will make you stronger and will help you be more of your Authentic Self, all that God intended you to be!

Open the door to love in all relationships.

Summary of Significant Points

1. The purpose of going through the process of clearing means that the frequency of your vibration is raised and your consciousness is expanded, creating more awareness.

2. Everything in life is about intention.

3. Enlightenment means that you have let go of all fear and all duality. Once you begin the process of allowing and surrendering to divine energies which represents divine guidance, you move down the golden pathway to become highly enlightened. Then you are on the fast track because you realize things are not real anymore—that it is all illusion and that you create your own reality.

4. You can rise above fear and realize that everything is a lesson for you. Things are not done to you; you are not a victim. You cause the things that happen to you. You are responsible for everything you have created. Part of stepping into enlightenment is not asking the question of why you may or may not have created something, but moving forward and creating something new.

5. Expand your I AM presence by moving into the divine flow—saying and doing that which comes from the heart.

6. Be kind and generous to your self, loving yourself more and more.

7. Utilize the Power of Your Intention:

I cannot overemphasize the necessity for you to begin to recognize how you create your world through intention. I urge you to change your vocabulary now and include words such as I am intending...I am manifesting...I choose to...I am bringing about... Delete the words "try" and "should" from your language now.

Sample Intentions:

- I intend to accelerate my personal evolution.
- I intend for Spirit to assist me in a greater capacity.
- I intend my body to be healthy, strong, and vibrant.
- I intend to release struggle and be a loving example to all I meet.
- I effortlessly intend that (<u>whatever you want</u>) comes about.

Gregg Braden suggested a four-step process in your intending which includes the following:

1. Honor all outcomes.

2. Give gratitude for the opportunity and ability to choose.

3. Visualize your chosen outcome in full and absolute detail.

4. Give gratitude for the blessing and joy the outcome brings.

Then you will intend a wonderful and amazing life for yourself.

Use the power of your mind to clearly intend what you want. Do you know how you want to feel? Find that feeling and then expand it. Ask for assistance from the nonphysical realms and visualize the outcome you would like to have. When you believe things are possible, your reality changes. Be aware that you have lots of unseen help just standing by waiting to be summoned or asked.

Music

Music is a wonderful way to uplift your Soul. The sounds and tones resonate through your body, and when you find something that works for you it has the power to really raise your vibration.

One of my favorite songs comes from Daniel Nahmod. An amazing poet, composer, and performer, Daniel's message is one of peace, love, and compassion:

Get ready, my Soul
I'm diving in
Get ready, my Soul
I'm diving in

To the deepest kind of love
To the sweetest kind of life
Get ready
Get ready, my Soul

Everything I've ever done
Everything I've ever seen
Everything I've lost or won
Everything I've ever dreamed
Has brought me here to the present moment
Here to a new beginning
Here and I'm seeing life so clearly now

Get ready, my Soul
I'm diving in
Get ready, my Soul
I'm diving in

To the deepest kind of love
To the sweetest kind of life
Get ready
Get ready, my Soul

'Cause here I go
Deeper, deeper, deeper than I've ever been before
Here I go
Closer, closer, closer to my sacred Source
Here I go
Deeper, deeper, deeper than I've every been before
Here I go
Closer, closer, closer to my sacred Source

Get ready, my Soul
I'm diving in
Get ready, my Soul
I'm diving in

To the deepest kind of love
To the sweetest kind of life
Get Ready
Get ready, my Soul

Get ready
Get ready, my Soul

Daniel Nahmod, from his CD, *Sacred Love: Songs for the New Worship Generation* www.danielnahmod.com

Exercise:

Find music that moves you, that speaks to you. Listen every day in your car or on your CD player or MP3 player.

See if you can get to the point that you wake up singing or feeling music move through you.

Affirmation:

I am a magnificent expression of Universal Intelligence.

I love unconditionally.

Love is the currency of my life.

CHAPTER TWELVE

Someday, after mastering the winds, the waves, the tides and gravity,
we shall harness for God the energies of love, and then,
for a second time in the history of the world,
man will have discovered fire.
Pierre Teilhard de Chardin

Living Daily In The Fifth

Because we are all different souls on different paths and no two DNA are the same we each have a different fifth dimension to anchor into our daily lives. In the beginning, going deeper and further establishing ourselves in the fifth dimensional requires a conscious intent. The fifth dimension starts internally before it ever manifest externally. When our frequencies or vibrations are completely fifth, then of course we are attracting only fifth dimensional experiences. If for some reason the fifth is not showing up around us then we have to go further inside ourselves. As Jesus said "The Kingdom of God is within." Here within we discover our authentic Divine self; the one who may have been hidden from us as we lived according to our outside world. We are allowing the world outside ourselves to guide us in fear and duality. No longer do we look to others for the answer to

"How shall I live my Life," others' happiness may not be our personal happiness. The work begins as we excavate our authentic self and connect with our divinity. Waking up to the truth of our being, may cause us to take action to remove ourselves from a place that does not match our truth. We learn to live daily in the fifth how by:

1. Feeling good and avoiding the negative thought or word.
2. Knowing that we have secure connection to our Divine Creator who only wants the very best for us.
3. Understanding that we do not see the whole picture and the consequences but all is in Divine Order for the highest and best for all concerned.
4. Giving thanks and appreciation for the Divine synchronicities and miraculous mani-festation in our daily lives.
5. Connecting with the energies of like-souls who want to share the joys of living and loving.
6. Staying centered in the knowledge that we are here for a Divine purpose, a mission, a job of great importance to the earth and the souls on the planet.
7. Understanding that each soul has a divine connection with the other. As people show up in our daily lives, they are important.

8. Staying in the moment to the awareness of your surroundings.

Our needs and desires begin to manifest easily without struggle or worry. We have every confirmation that our needs are known even before we ask and we are cared for by a power who wants to love us as we love ourselves and others. We learn that to live any other way than in bliss is not acceptable. When we feel surrounded by irritants, we simply learn to step away to another direction. If I am living in divine order then the irritants are there to get my attention. Today while reading an email from someone it felt harsh and then I realized that they were creating in the third dimension of fear and duality. This person was responding to me in fear and not in love, so what should I do? What feelings are coming up in me from their words? Is it something that needs my attention or showing me how to recognize and dodge these lower frequencies? Now I had to show and feel gratitude for the lesson.

The more awakened I became; the more I realized that my surroundings did not match the authentic self I had discovered. My desire was to live closer to nature and God, with a slower pace, under a great big sky. I packed my van and drove west. I had to move forward and leave my old life behind, taking no one with me; I followed the Divine Will of my soul. I moved from Georgia, where I spent most all my sixty years, to live in New Mexico; Land of Enchantment. One year ago I knew no one here, and then clients and events led me to come and work in New Mexico for two weeks. I knew this was my true home and the place my soul longed to be. I no longer had to search for a parking lot so I could sit and look up at a full sky. This land is all about a fulll sky and that causes me to have the sweetest peaceful feeling of being so close to Divinity. I live in a village of fourteen hundred people where the shopping is sixty miles away. Everyone is important here because there are so few of us.

In the evening I stand on a bridge over the Pecos River and watch a spectacular light show in the sky call the 'setting sun.' I never tire of this event that happens every evening nor do I tire of the many animals who also call this place their home.

As I live in this oasis in the middle of the desert, I know that I am cared for in every way. I am reminded of the fairy tales I heard as a child, magic happens and they live happily ever after. As a small child I longed for that magical place where I could live happily ever after. I did question God along the way, once you start on the journey of surrendering to the Divine path you obey, never question only trust that clear voice of intuition to guide you. There is no turning back, only letting go of more and more.

One day you sit observing and noticing that life has changed one hundred degrees and who else but God could have orchestrated this?

Now Is The Time

by Patricia Diane Cota-Robles
http://eraofpeace.org

We have all heard the Hopi quote, "We are the Ones we have been waiting for." Never in recorded history has that statement meant more or been more accurate than during this Cosmic Moment. This is a critical time in the evolution of this planet, and we are witnessing the most intensified cleansing process Humanity has ever experienced. We have all heard the saying "You cannot pour new wine into old bottles, lest the new wine becomes contaminated." That is a powerful metaphor for what is occurring on Earth at this moment. In order for our NEW planetary CAUSE of Divine Love to physically manifest on Earth, we must first transmute all of the human miscreations that conflict with Divine Love.

According to the Company of Heaven, 2011 is an auspicious year that is moving the Earth and all her Life up the spiral of evolution into frequencies of God's Transfiguring Divine Love beyond anything we have ever experienced. Myriad activities of Light will occur this year that are

Divinely Designed to prepare every particle of Life on Earth to withstand this increased frequency of Divine Love at an atomic, cellular level. Our Father-Mother God and the Company of Heaven want this influx of Divine Love to assist Humanity in ways that will enhance our Earthly experience, not wreak havoc in our lives. This purging process a critical step in our Ascension process, and it is preparing Humanity at a cellular level for the unprecedented influx of Light that is destined to occur throughout the remainder of 2011 and 2012.

2011 is being heralded as "The Transfiguring Year of Rebirth and Renewal." This will be brought to fruition through the unified efforts of Humanity and the Company of Heaven. This means that you and I and every other awakened person on the planet have the responsibility of being the Open Door for this influx of Divine Love. We will succeed in this monumental mission through various activities of Light that we will be called to participate in by our I AM Presence.

Humanity is being provided with opportunities beyond anything we have ever experienced. This Truth is resonating in every Heart Flame, and people everywhere are beginning to sense the magnitude of the hour. People in every walk of life are awakening and they are beginning "to see with new eyes and hear with new ears." We have all been preparing for aeons of time to fulfill our unique facets of this Divine Plan. Now our I AM Presence is calling us to our highest service ever.

If you are networking on the Internet or communicating with people around the world, you know that there are all kinds of reports of cataclysmic earth changes being predicted. These reports are coming from every conceivable source, including some ancient, indigenous cultures, as well as some scientific forecasts.

This revivified interest in dramatic earth changes is not occurring by chance. In fact, a cataclysmic purging is exactly what was expected to occur in the original Divine Plan after the Shift of the Ages. That type of cleansing was thought to be a necessary factor in creating the environment for Earth's Ascension, so the old Earth could pass away. Now people are tuning in to those obsolete predictions and reporting them as though they are still destined to occur. However, that is not the case. Everything has changed. Those old predictions are no longer viable, and the cataclysmic earth changes are no longer necessary. Now there is a powerful contingency plan in place that was cocreated over the past 30 years by Lightworkers around the world who were working in unison with the Company of Heaven.

The old Earth is not going to pass away! The two Earths have become ONE, and EVERY person evolving on this planet has made the conscious choice, through his or her I AM Presence, to do what is necessary in order to clear their karmic liabilities and Ascend into the 5th Dimension. This is a miracle beyond our comprehension, but it is a profound Truth that has been revealed to Humanity by the Company of Heaven.

Since the monumental influx of Divine Consciousness that took place during Harmonic Concordance in November 2003, Humanity's I AM Presence has greater access to our heart and mind. This glorious aspect of our own Divinity can now work through us in previously unknown ways, as we volunteer to assist in the healing process that is now unfolding on Earth.

Our thoughts and feelings are creative, so it is vital that Lightworkers join together to transmute the negative predictions of destruction and death being buffeted about via the media and the Internet. People who are reporting these cataclysmic events are tapping into obsolete, etheric records that no longer serve the highest good for this planet. The underlying intent is to keep Humanity so paralyzed by fear that we will not be able to assimilate and integrate our NEW planetary CAUSE of Divine Love, Oneness, and Reverence for Life.

The Earth is a living, breathing organism, and she is going to cleanse and purge herself of the atrocities Humanity has inflicted upon her. The important thing to understand is that **this cleansing can be done through Light and an influx of Divine Love rather than through destructive earth changes.** That is where the Lightworkers come into the picture. We are now being called to a new level of Divine Service.

During the time between the December 21, 2010 Solstice, and the Full Moon Lunar Eclipse that took place on that day, and the New Moon Solar Eclipse on January 4, 2011, hundreds of thousands of Lightworkers around the world joined Heart Flames and created a New Planetary CAUSE of Divine Love in the Realms of Cause. This powerful influx of Light is now blazing through the Heart Flames of embodied Lightworkers and gradually piercing into the core of purity in every electron of precious Life energy on Earth. Everything that conflicts with Divine Love is now being pushed to the surface at an accelerated pace to be healed and transmuted back into Light. This is causing a great deal of stress in the body of Mother Earth which needs to be addressed by you and me and every conscious person around the world.

At this very moment, radical, revolutionary, overnight change is more possible than ever before. Humanity's collective shift into a consciousness of Divine Love, Oneness, and Reverence for ALL Life is now not only viable, but a very real and tangible option. Miraculous changes are daily and hourly taking place within every man, woman, and child. As we each, with clear intent, focus on our personal and planetary Transfiguration, Rebirth, and Renewal, our victory is assured.

With the accelerated influx of God's Divine Love, Humanity's Spiritual Brain Centers are being activated. As Divine Love filters into our outer minds our I AM Presence is releasing new visions of possibility to us in which the Oneness of Life, Peace, Abundance, and Freedom are attainable realities and Reverence for Life is the order of the New Day.

Our newly activated 5th-Dimensional Solar Chakras are enabling the physiological aspects of the 3rd and 4th Dimensions to be lifted into and merged with the multidimensional aspects of the Infinite Physical Perfection in the 5th Dimension. This process is reordering our DNA into new expressions of eternal youth, vibrant health, and infinite perfection. These expressions are the natural reflection of our physical, etheric, mental, and emotional Solar Light Bodies. This event is creating a deep stirring and change within each of us. Suddenly and miraculously, nothing is the same.

Now it is time for us to utilize our new, sacred gifts of transformation for the benefit of Humanity and all Life evolving on this blessed planet. The Beings of Light in the Realms of Illumined Truth are invoking our assistance in another vitally important facet of the Divine Plan. Please go within and kneel before the altar of Divine Love blazing in your heart. Listen for the still, small voice of your inner guidance, and respond to this Clarion Call according to the directives of your God Self.

The key factors in Humanity's ultimate awakening involve the remembrance of our Oneness with ALL Life and the healing of the atrocities we have inflicted on Mother Earth. Your heart commitment and your dedication to the Light are vitally important factors in helping to heal Humanity's separation from God and the body of Mother Earth. If this were not the case, your I AM Presence would not have magnetized this information into your sphere of awareness.

The NEED OF THE HOUR is for awakened Lightworkers to join hearts and minds as we cocreate a living, ever-expanding Forcefield of the Violet Flame that will transmute the surfacing negativity and reinforce the vulnerable areas in the body of Mother Earth. The reason the Company of Heaven has assured us that the cataclysmic earth changes that were originally predicted are no longer necessary is because they are aware of the heart commitment of you, and me, and the millions of people all over the world who are willing to invoke the Violet Flame on behalf of Humanity and Mother Earth. **Yes indeed! We ARE the Ones we have been waiting for.**

Know that Light is infinitely more powerful than fear. ONE Lightworker focusing effectively on the Light can release enough positive energy to counteract the fragmented, fear-based, hate-filled thoughts and feelings of literally hundreds of thousands of people. In addition to that blessing, the Beings of Light have been given Cosmic Dispensation by our Father-Mother God. They have been granted permission to amplify our unified efforts a thousand times a thousandfold. Consequently, the critical mass of Heaven on Earth is much, much closer than it appears.

The following invocation is specifically designed to help awaken every recalcitrant soul and to assist every neophyte and awakened soul to integrate the new frequencies of Divine Love quickly and effortlessly. It is also designed to reinforce the vulnerable areas in the body of Mother Earth in order to avert the potential of cataclysmic earth changes.

As this Forcefield of Light is empowered each day through the thoughts, words, actions and feelings of Lightworkers around the world, its effect will be exponential, and the Light of Divine Love and planetary healing will penetrate quickly into every person's conscious and subconscious mind.

Now, let's join our hearts with the I AM Presence of every man, woman, and child on Earth, the entire Company of Heaven, and the Legions of Light associated with the 5th-Dimensional Violet Flame of God's Infinite Perfection.

Violet Flame of 1,000 Suns

I AM my I AM Presence, and I AM One with the I AM Presence of every person on Earth. I AM also One with my Father-Mother God and the entire Company of Heaven. Now as one voice, one heartbeat, one breath, and one energy, vibration, and consciousness of pure Divine Love we invoke the most intensified frequencies of God's Violet Flame of Infinite Perfection that the Earth and Humanity are capable of receiving at this time.

We open the Stargates of our Hearts, and we are instantly the Open Door for the most powerful 5th-Dimensional frequencies of the Violet Flame of God's Infinite Perfection the Earth has ever experienced.

The Violet Flame pulsates through our Heart Flames and blazes in, through, and around all inharmonious actions, all lower human conscious- ness and all obstructions of the Light that any per- son, place, condition, or thing has ever placed in the pathway of Life's perfection.

Instantly, the Violet Flame Transmutes this dis- cordant energy cause, core, effect, record, and memory back into its original perfection.

Now Violet Fire Angels take their strategic posi- tions over every country, state, city, town, village, and hamlet on the planet. These selfless messen- gers of our Father-Mother God reach out their great loving arms and raise up a limitless number of people in every location who are willing to par- ticipate in the faithful use of the Violet Flame of God's Infinite Perfection. Each of these people understand the full importance of the Violet Flame now being offered by our Father-Mother God to help free Humanity from all human distresses.

The conscious use of this mighty power from the Heart of God will cause to be established within every one of these places great foci of the Violet Flame, which will continually bathe every person in each vicinity until Humanity's human miscrea- tions are transmuted back into Light and the body of Mother Earth is healed and restored to her original perfection.

Now, through the Clarion Call of the I AM Presence of ALL Humanity and the Legions of Light throughout infinity, the Violet Flame begins to expand and expand. It merges with the Immortal Victorious Threefold Flame blazing in every person's heart and explodes into a tremendous Starburst of Light.

This miraculous influx of the Violet Flame increases to the intensity and power of a thousand Suns.

Beloved Legions of Light associated with the 5th-Dimensional Violet Flame of God's Infinite Perfection...

a) Blaze the Light of a thousand Suns through the physical, etheric, mental, and emotional strata within the bodies of Mother Earth until the elements of earth, air, water, fire, and ether are purified and restored to their pristine beauty.

b) Blaze the Light of a thousand Suns through all of the vulnerable areas in the body of Mother Earth. Reinforce with bolts of Violet Lightning all of the faults, cracks, fissures, tectonic plates, and the wounds created in the body of Mother Earth through nuclear testing, mining, drilling for oil, and every other human affliction.

c) Blaze the Light of a thousand Suns through the thoughts, words, actions, and feelings of every man, woman, and child evolving on Earth until every person individually acknowledges and accepts the Oneness of ALL Life, and every expression reflects the Reverence of ALL Life.

d) Blaze the Light of a thousand Suns through all incoming babies, the children, their parents, and guardians until ALL youth are raised up in energy, vibration, and consciousness to carry out the directives of their I AM Presence.

e) Blaze the Light of a thousand Suns through all youth centers and activities, all schools, colleges, and universities, all leaders, teachers, instructors, and professors in every line of endeavor until the Flame of God Illumination and Enlightenment is manifest and eternally sustained.

f) Blaze the Light of a thousand Suns through all religions and spiritual teachings, so that Divine Love, Truth, Tolerance, and Universal Sisterhood and Brotherhood will quickly manifest.

g) Blaze the Light of a thousand Suns through all doctors, nurses, healers, hospitals, insurance companies, pharmaceutical conglomerates, and every institution associated with healing of any kind until Divine Mercy, Healing, Compassion, and Vibrant Health are tangible realities for every evolving soul.

h) Blaze the Light of a thousand Suns through all banking and financial institutions, all economic systems, all money, and the people associated with monetary interactions of any kind until every person on Earth is openly demonstrating true integrity, honesty, generosity, fairness, abundance, and the God supply of all good things.

i) Blaze the Light of a thousand Suns through all places of incarceration and all employed there, through every correctional institution, all law enforcement personnel, every judge, jury, and court of law until Divine Justice is manifest and eternally sustained.

j) Blaze the Light of a thousand Suns through all space activities throughout the world until every nation unites in cooperative service, so that God's Will may be manifest with our sisters and brothers throughout the Universe.

k) Blaze the Light of a thousand Suns through the physical, etheric, mental, and emotional bodies of Humanity until all disease and human miscreation, its cause and core, is dissolved and transmuted into vibrant health, eternal youth, and physical perfection.

l) Blaze the Light of a thousand Suns through the food and water industries and through all of the food and water used for human consumption until every particle of food and every molecule of water is filled with Light. Empower this Elemental substance to raise the vibratory action of Humanity's physical, etheric, mental, and emotional bodies until physical perfection becomes a sustained manifest reality for every Human Being.

m) Blaze the Light of a thousand Suns in, through, and around every remaining electron of precious Life energy until the Immaculate Concept of the New Earth is manifest, and all Life evolving here is wholly Ascended and FREE. And so it is.

Patricia Diane Cota-Robles
New Age Study of Humanity's Purpose
a 501 (c) 3 nonprofit educational organization
http://eraofpeace.org

FAX: 520.751.2981
Phone: 520.885.7909
New Age Study of Humanity's Purpose
PO Box 41883,
Tucson, Arizona 85717

This article is copyrighted, but you have my permission to share it through any medium as long as it is not altered and the proper credit line is included.

©2011 Patricia Diane Cota-Robles

Resources

———————◼———————

Great men are they who see that spiritual is stronger
than material force, that thoughts rule the world.

Ralph Waldo Emerson

There are many who propose to channel higher beings and expound upon the coming times and their meaning. There are also many books, websites, and seminars that inform and teach varied perspectives. It is by no means a complete list of everything that is available on the Internet or in the marketplace. Please be advised that I do not evaluate, judge, or recommend. Feel free to explore any and all of these resources, but trust the truth of who you are within. Learn to discern. Take what is helpful to you and disregard the rest. The highest truth resides within you and you may trust that over any one else's opinion.

Books Recommended for Further Study and Associated Websites

Bishop, Karen. *Remembering Your Soul Purpose*, 2nd ed. USA: Bookkeepers.com, Inc., 2006.

_____. *Stepping Into the New Reality*. USA: Bookkeepers.com, Inc., 2008.

http://www.emergingearthangels.com

Bonnell, Gary. *The Twelve Days of Light: Prophecy Concerning the Millennium.*

Atlanta: Richman Rose Publishing, 1998.

Braden, Gregg. *Awakening to Zero Point: The Collective Initiation, Sacred Spaces, Ancient Wisdom*, 2nd ed. New York: Three Rivers Press, 1997.

_____. *The Isaiah Effect: Decoding The Lost Science of Prayer and Prophecy*. New York: Three Rivers Press, 2000.

_____. *The God Code: The Secret of Our Past, the Promise of Our Future*. Carlsbad: Hay House, 2004.

_____. *The Divine Matrix: Bridging Time, Space, Miracles, and Belief*. Carlsbad: Hay House, 2007.

http://greggbraden.com

Brewer, Ann. *The Power of Twelve: A New Approach to Personal Empowerment*. Fairfield: Sunstar Publishing, 1999.

http://www.annebrewer.com

Clow, Barbara Hand with Gerry Clow. *Alchemy of Nine Dimensions: Decoding the Vertical Axis, Crop Circles, and the Mayan Calendar*. Charlottesville: Hampton Roads, 2004.

http://www.handclow2012.com

Gawain, Shakti. *Living in the Light*, revised edition. Novato: Nataraj Publishing, 1998.

http://www.shaktigawain.com

Gerard, Dr. Robert V. *Change Your DNA, Change Your Life!* Binghamton: Oughten House Foundation, 2002.

http://www.oughtenhouse.com/ohi.php

Hicks, Esther and Jerry Hicks. *Ask and It is Given: Learning How to Manifest Your Desires*. Carlsbad: Hay House, Inc., 2004.

http://www.abraham-hicks.com

Joudry, Patricia and Maurie D. Pressman, M.D. *Twin Souls: Finding Your True Spiritual Partner.* Center City: Hazelden, 2000.

http://www.soundtherapyinternational.com/v3/home.html

http://www.mauriepressman.com

Kaa, Sri Ram and Kira Raa. *2012 Awakening.* Berkeley: Ulysses Press, 2008.

http://www.selfascension.com

Klein, Eric. *The Inner Door: Channeled Discourses from the Ascended Masters on Self-Mastery and Ascension.* Binghamton: : Oughten House Publishers, 1993.

MacLaine, Shirley. *The Camino: A Journey of the Spirit.* New York: Pocket Books, 2000.

http://www.shirleymaclaine.com

Marciniak, Barbara. *Bringers of the Dawn.* Rochester:: Bear & Company, 1992.

_____. *Family of Light.* Rochester: Bear & Company, 1999.

_____. *Path to Empowerment.* Makawao: Inner Ocean Publishing, 2004.

http://www.pleiadians.com

McCannon, Tricia. *Dialogues with the Angels.* Atlanta: Horizons Unlimited, Inc., 1996.

_____. *Jesus: The Explosive Story of the 30 Lost Years and The Ancient Mystery Religions.* Charlottesville: Hampton Roads, 2010.

http://www.triciamccannonspeaks.com

Mirdad, Michael. *The Seven Initiations of the Spiritual Path: Understanding the Purpose of Life's Tests.* Bellingham: Grail Productions, 2003.

http://www.grailproductions.com

Munro, Wendy. *Journey Into the New Millennium: A Cosmic Account of the Millennial Transformation for Humanity and Planet Earth.* QLD, Australia: Triad Publications, 1997.

Perala, Robert with Tony Stubbs. *The Divine Blueprint: Roadmap for the New Millennium.* Scotts Valley: United Light Publishing, 2001.

http://www.lightstreamers.com/perala.htm

Ruiz, Don Miguel. *The Four Agreements*. San Rafael: Amber Allen Publishing, 1997.

http://www.miguelruiz.com/

Self, Jim and Roxane Burnett. *Spirit Matters: Down to Earth Tools for A Spirited Life*, 2nd ed. Boise: Tree of Life Press, 2008.

http://masteringalchemy.com

Sterling, Fred. *Kireal: The Great Shift*. Binghamton: Oughten House Publishers, 1998.

http://www.kirael.com

Stevenson, Sandy. *The Awakener: The Time is Now*. Bath, UK: Gateway Books, 1997.

http://lightascension.com

Stone, Joshua David. *Revelations of a Melchizedek Initiate (Easy-To-Read Encyclopedia of the Spiritual Path)*. Sedona: Light Technology Publishing, 1998.

_____. *Golden Keys to Ascension and Healing: Revelations of Sai Baba and the Ascended Masters (Easy-To-Read Encyclopedia of the Spiritual Path)*. Sedona: Light Technology Publishing, 1998.

_____. *Hidden Mysteries: ET's, Ancient Mystery Schools and Ascension, (The Easy-to-Read Encyclopedia of the Spiritual Path, Volume IV)*. Sedona: Light Technology Publishing, 1997.

http://www.iamuniversity.org

Stone, Wistancia. *Invocations to the Light*. Nevada City: Blue Dolphin Publishing, 1999.

http://www.wistancia.com/index1.html

Tachi-ren, Tashira (Archangel Ariel). *What is Lightbody?* 3rd ed. Lithia Springs: New Leaf Distribution, 1999.

http://www.alchemicalmage.com/associates. htm

Tolle, Eckhart. *A New Earth: Awakening To Your Life's Purpose*. New York: A Plume Book, 2005.

http://www.eckharttolle.com

Virtue, Doreen. *Archangels & Ascended Maters: A Guide to Working and Healing with Divinities and Deities*. Carlsbad: Hay House, 2003.

_____. *Goddesses & Angels: Awakening Your Inner High-Priestess and "Source-eress."* Carlsbad: Hay House, 2005.

_____. *Divine Magic: The Seven Sacred Secrets of Manifestation.* Carlsbad: Hay House, Inc., 2006.

http://www.angeltherapy.com

Wilde, Stuart. *Sixth Sense: Including the Secret of the Etheric Subtle Body.* Carlsbad: Hay House, 2000.

_____. *The Three Keys to Self Empowerment.* Carlsbad: Hay House, 2004.

http://www.stuartwilde.com

Wright, Machaelle Small. *MAP: Medical Assistance Program.* Warrenton: Perelandra, Ltd., 1994.

http://www.perelandra-ltd.com

Additional Websites You May Wish to Visit

www.eraofpeace.org

Patricia Diane Cota-Robles

Patricia is cofounder and president of the non-profit, educational organization New Age Study of Humanity's Purpose, Inc., which sponsors the Annual World Congress On Illumination.

The Divine Intent of the Celestial Sharings on her website is to give Humanity greater clarity and understanding, as we progress through these wondrous but extremely challenging times on Earth.

http://sirianrevelations.net

Patricia Cori is a highly regarded clairvoyant/ channel. She is a master teacher and author of several books on Sirian revelation.

http://newearthsummit.org

A free public discussion forum that includes various thematic boards relating to the beginning of our awakening to our true nature and destiny.

http://www.glcoherence.org

The Global Coherence Initiative is a science-based initiative to unite millions of people in heart-focused care and intention—to shift global consciousness from instability and discord to balance, cooperation, and enduring peace.

www.the2012countdown.com

Includes channeling from Carolyn Evers and information from Dr. Richard Presser about the coming events on all different levels.

http://www.inspirationandintuition.com

Darlene Pitts's website is filled with inspiration and provides empowering and life-changing inspirational and intuition services and products.

About the Author

CINDY BENTLEY

As a healer, teacher, and leader, Cindy's passions have been metaphysics and healing from a very early age. For many years this was expressed through her professional career in the traditional medical field as a Registered Nurse. Now she knows her nursing career was a prelude to her true mission. As a nurse she felt called to nurture and heal the physical body of her patients; as an energy practitioner she works to heal *all* the energy bodies.

It was after reading Anne Brewer's book **The Power of Twelve** that Cindy became cognizant of the work she was to do. She stepped into her purpose as a Lightworker and today deeply feels her mission is to help heal and activate our DNA in preparation for the shift that is almost upon us. After an extensive apprenticeship during which she learned to clear and perform blueprint repatterning she became a spiritual energy cleaner who removes the dark clutter that blocks us from receiving and holding Divine Light.

In her work she acts as a catalyst for people to recognize that they are not alone. With the help of the Divine Creator, Ascended Masters, and Archangels she works to remove negative energies throughout our bodies and all energy fields. Her work speeds up the process of reconnection and healing of the twelve strands of DNA.

Her intention is to touch the hearts and minds of other Lightworkers who have not yet awakened so that they may become cognizant of their mission on the planet right now.

Contact Cindy

cbentleyrn@aol.com

Cindy Bentley
7113 Call Jenah
Santa Fe, New Mexico 87507

www.cindybentley.com
www.DNAreconnection.com

Testimonials

—————■—————

"In each of our lives, we experience certain individuals who seem to grasp the greater truth of their existence. Those of us who are fortunate enough to recognize these souls are given the opportunity to delve into a deep connection with self, our creator, and one another. One such human being whom I am gifted to know is Cindy Bentley. Through deep prayer, meditation, and introspection, Cindy connects to her inner truth and helps others to align and clear any impediments blocking them from achieving their true life purpose. With grace and humility, Cindy opens her heart to assist others along their path toward achieving their innermost connection to self."
—Marigrace

"Since working with Cindy, my dreams are now at an epic scale with such details and substance like never before. For about a year and a half I have suffered with severe headaches every week. They are now very rare and just faint. I have also found a job." —Larry Hartwell

"I have been to many Holistic Practitioners and find Cindy to be professional, loving, and having amazing capabilities. She was able to accomplish clearing work in my home that others could not. I am feeling peace, happiness, and better focus since my clearing with her." —Kimberly

"I have felt the benefits from Cindy's energy work profoundly. Every day I am opening up to higher levels of consciousness and spirituality. I recommended Cindy to many of my friends who I felt were ready for the next step in their spiritual journeys." —Sandy

"Cindy Bentley is truly a Godsend! I prayed for help at a time when I was lonely depressed and struggling to find my balance and myself again. After having Cindy work on me I felt whole again. Her healing work continues to bless my life with the strength to overcome all of life's lessons. I thank God everyday for putting her in my path." —Lucy

"Thanks for a wonderful clearing, cleansing, and dynamic blessing last Thursday. I feel energized and very much at peace. It was a joy to work with you, chat with you, and be with you. Take care and keep in touch." —Dede

"Thank you, Cindy, for opening me up to a new life and being a part of my journey." —Shayna.

"It's been four days and so far so good. The first night I was sleepy; although, I still did not sleep deeply. My body was also very warm that night. Another change is that I haven't been as tired while at work and I'm more focused. Finally, my body is really light. There are moments when I don't feel like I weigh anything. I only feel my body after eating." —Kevin

"Hope you are doing well! I am feeling so much better. I have to tell you that I had two lumps in one of my breasts. They have been there for years and I keep checking them and have had a couple of mammograms. They are totally gone!!!! I am so glad our paths have crossed. Thank you!!!!" —Brenda, Ashville.

"I can't tell you how much I enjoyed our session. It has changed my life! You wouldn't believe the changes in my husband as well. I did not tell him anything of what I had done, as I wasn't sure what he would think. So...all is well in the Family!" —Patricia

"First, I just have to tell you how much you mean in my life and how much my life has changed since my first visit with you. You have made such an incredible difference and I absolutely cherish having you in my life. I would not at all be where I am today—spiritually or emotionally. So thank you so much for the difference you are making in my world, as well as so many other worlds." —Linda

"Your words make me cry with Joy. Thank you, Cindy." —Allison

"Thank you for your help. We did call those you named in and burnt everything to complete ashes. Strangely, the whole time we burned, there were several coyotes howling in the distance non-stop.

As soon as the fire was out, they stopped! For the first time in weeks, I slept through the night and the night after that! I feel much freer now and it has made an amazing difference on the way I've been working on my book. I truly feel guided by a higher power with it. It's as if I am only seeing through one eye and someone else is guiding me through the other, which blurs out completely. Everything has a strange white glow around it when I'm working. I'm in a completely different space. Gary could feel in my muscles during a massage last night that I seemed much "lighter." What a relief it has to have that negative part of my life gone forever! So, again, thank you! The work you are doing is so important and I hope it brings you and those you heal much joy." —Christine

"Wanted to let you know my husband received a very large and unexpected bonus as work last week!!!! I asked the pendulum if this was a result of your healing, and it said yes!!! Anyway, we continue to be blessed by your great work and healing powers. I continue to tell everyone of your great work and what a wonderful gift your healing is. I am so very grateful for you." —Priscilla

"I felt wonderful and more free and clear after just one session with you. Thank you so much, Cindy. You are truly a wonderful old soul and a gift from God at a time when the world truly needs it." —Darlene

"I feel like I've been touched by an angel."

"Jodie is doing great and she LOVED meeting with you when it was all said and done. I had to make her go kicking and screaming inside herself, but I knew it was best to get the little bit of dark out of her. She has everything you gave her in a locked box in her room. She said she is going to write a book and you will be in it...lol. She said thank you mama for making me go...I really liked that lady. Anyway, thank you again. I can feel her new angels around her. What a Joy. Make sure you clear yourself today and no issues can bring you down to earth!!!! You are truly a Gift from God." —Cindy

"Cindy performed some prayer work on me back in the spring. I really didn't totally understand about all the reasons that she was doing it. She called it clearing. I called it prayer. I knew that Cindy was very loving, full of the Holy Spirit and a powerful, gifted healer. After the clearing, I was very sick for about a week to fourteen days. I didn't feel well, and I couldn't eat. I just drank lots of water and ate very little. I felt in my spirit that I was being healed and cleansed in spirit, body and mind—present past and future. I know that it is God's love and power working through Cindy that has given her a willing heart and the courage to step out and accept this high calling for her life." —Debra Rose

"I am still having a little trouble with that one tooth, but it keeps getting better each day, so it is probably fine. I have no idea why I was in such pain with it. I have noticed my intuition is stronger and have had some amazing little 'feelings' that seem totally off the wall, but I follow them and it makes sense later. I have noticed my thoughts/desires becoming manifest very quickly! I am amazed and thought it was just coincidence the first few times, but it keeps happening. Wow. What amazing work GOD is doing through you." — Brenda, Ashville

"I just saw your ad in the *Oracle* magazine. Good for you. Over the past three years, I have become very involved in metaphysics. My spirituality is the most important aspect of my life. You were a primary influence for me to feel and see the light. Thank you for helping me in the past. I enjoyed and appreciate the books that you gave me. I going to Kennesaw University and still have trouble from time to time, but I am transforming." —Jessie

64967516R00165

Made in the USA
Lexington, KY
26 June 2017